DEEP LEARNING

COMPUTER VISION, PYTHON MACHINE LEARNING AND NEURAL NETWORKS

4 BOOKS IN 1

BOOK 1
DEEP LEARNING DEMYSTIFIED: A BEGINNER'S GUIDE

BOOK 2
MASTERING COMPUTER VISION WITH DEEP LEARNING

BOOK 3
PYTHON MACHINE LEARNING AND NEURAL NETWORKS: FROM NOVICE TO PRO

BOOK 4
ADVANCED DEEP LEARNING: CUTTING-EDGE TECHNIQUES AND APPLICATIONS

ROB BOTWRIGHT

Published by Rob Botwright
Library of Congress Cataloging-in-Publication Data
ISBN 978-1-83938-626-8
Cover design by Rizzo

Disclaimer

The contents of this book are based on extensive research and the best available historical sources. However, the author and publisher make no claims, promises, or guarantees about the accuracy, completeness, or adequacy of the information contained herein. The information in this book is provided on an "as is" basis, and the author and publisher disclaim any and all liability for any errors, omissions, or inaccuracies in the information or for any actions taken in reliance on such information. The opinions and views expressed in this book are those of the author and do not necessarily reflect the official policy or position of any organization or individual mentioned in this book. Any reference to specific people, places, or events is intended only to provide historical context and is not intended to defame or malign any group, individual, or entity. The information in this book is intended for educational and entertainment purposes only. It is not intended to be a substitute for professional advice or judgment. Readers are encouraged to conduct their own research and to seek professional advice where appropriate. Every effort has been made to obtain necessary permissions and acknowledgments for all images and other copyrighted material used in this book. Any errors or omissions in this regard are unintentional, and the author and publisher will correct them in future editions.

BOOK 1 - DEEP LEARNING DEMYSTIFIED: A BEGINNER'S GUIDE

BOOK 2 - MASTERING COMPUTER VISION WITH DEEP LEARNING

BOOK 3 - PYTHON MACHINE LEARNING AND NEURAL NETWORKS: FROM NOVICE TO PRO

BOOK 4 - ADVANCED DEEP LEARNING: CUTTING-EDGE TECHNIQUES AND APPLICATIONS

Introduction

Welcome to the exciting world of "DEEP LEARNING: COMPUTER VISION, PYTHON MACHINE LEARNING AND NEURAL NETWORKS." In this transformative book bundle, we embark on a captivating journey through the realms of artificial intelligence, deep learning, computer vision, and the intricate world of neural networks.

Our book bundle is designed to cater to a wide spectrum of readers, from those taking their first steps into the world of AI to seasoned professionals looking to master advanced techniques. We have carefully curated four distinct volumes, each offering a unique perspective and expertise:

BOOK 1 - DEEP LEARNING DEMYSTIFIED: A BEGINNER'S GUIDE
In this foundational volume, we lay the groundwork for your deep learning journey. Starting from scratch, we demystify complex concepts and make them accessible to beginners. Through clear explanations and hands-on examples, you'll gain a solid understanding of neural networks, activation functions, and the fundamentals of Python programming.

BOOK 2 - MASTERING COMPUTER VISION WITH DEEP LEARNING Building on your newfound knowledge, this book takes you on a captivating exploration of computer vision. Dive into the world of image processing, convolutional neural networks (CNNs), and the art of recognizing objects in images. By mastering these techniques, you'll be equipped to create intelligent vision-based applications with confidence.

BOOK 3 - PYTHON MACHINE LEARNING AND NEURAL NETWORKS: FROM NOVICE TO PRO Our third volume elevates your skills by introducing you to the diverse landscape of machine learning and neural networks. Learn the essentials of data preprocessing, delve into supervised and unsupervised learning algorithms, and discover the power of training neural networks. From novices to proficient practitioners, this book covers it all.

BOOK 4 - ADVANCED DEEP LEARNING: CUTTING-EDGE TECHNIQUES AND APPLICATIONS As you progress through the bundle, our final volume opens the doors to advanced deep learning techniques. Explore optimization strategies, transfer learning, and conquer common deep learning challenges. The book culminates with a glimpse into real-world applications and emerging trends that are shaping the future of deep learning.

Whether you are a beginner eager to unlock the mysteries of AI, an intermediate learner seeking to expand your skill set, or an expert looking to stay at the forefront of the field, this book bundle offers something valuable for everyone. Each volume is crafted to empower you with knowledge, skills, and insights that will fuel your journey in the world of deep learning.

Join us on this exhilarating expedition as we unravel the complexities of AI, venture into the depths of neural networks, and witness the transformative impact of deep learning in various domains. With these four books as your guides, you're poised to embark on an educational adventure that will redefine your understanding of artificial intelligence and its limitless possibilities. Let's begin this extraordinary journey together.

BOOK 1
DEEP LEARNING DEMYSTIFIED
A BEGINNER'S GUIDE

ROB BOTWRIGHT

Chapter 1: Introduction to Deep Learning

Machine learning is a rapidly evolving field with applications spanning from self-driving cars to healthcare. It is essential to understand the fundamental principles that underlie this technology. At its core, machine learning is about creating algorithms that can learn from data and make predictions or decisions based on that data. These algorithms, often referred to as models, have the ability to improve their performance over time as they are exposed to more data. This capability is what sets machine learning apart from traditional rule-based programming.

To grasp the basics of machine learning, it's important to first understand the key components of the process. Data is the foundation upon which all machine learning models are built. This data can come in various forms, including text, images, numbers, or any combination of these. The quality and quantity of data are critical factors that can significantly impact the performance of a machine learning model.

Once you have the data, the next step is to preprocess it. Data preprocessing involves tasks such as cleaning, transforming, and encoding the data to make it suitable for the machine learning algorithms. Cleaning may involve handling missing values, removing outliers, and dealing with noisy data. Transformation can include scaling features to a common range or encoding categorical variables into numerical representations.

After preprocessing, the data is typically split into two subsets: the training set and the testing set. The training set is used to train the machine learning model, while the testing set is reserved for evaluating its performance. This separation ensures that the model's performance can be assessed on data it has never seen before, providing a measure of its generalization ability.

Now, it's time to choose a machine learning algorithm that suits the task at hand. There are various types of machine learning algorithms, including supervised learning, unsupervised learning, and reinforcement learning. Supervised learning involves training a model on labeled data, where the correct outcomes or labels are provided. This type of learning is commonly used for tasks like classification and regression.

Unsupervised learning, on the other hand, deals with unlabeled data and aims to find patterns or groupings within the data. Clustering and dimensionality reduction are common applications of unsupervised learning. Reinforcement learning focuses on training agents to make sequential decisions in an environment to maximize a reward. This is prevalent in applications like game playing and robotics.

Once an algorithm is selected, it's time to train the model. During training, the algorithm learns the underlying patterns and relationships within the data. It iteratively adjusts its internal parameters to minimize a specific objective function, such as mean squared error for regression or cross-entropy for classification. This process involves feeding the training data through the model multiple times, with each iteration leading to better model performance.

Evaluation is a critical step in assessing the model's quality. This is done using the testing set, which the model has not seen during training. Various metrics, such as accuracy, precision, recall, and F1-score for classification tasks, or mean squared error for regression tasks, can be used to measure the model's performance. The goal is to ensure that the model generalizes well to new, unseen data.

Machine learning is not a one-size-fits-all approach, and the choice of algorithm and model architecture depends on the specific problem you are trying to solve. Neural networks, particularly deep neural networks, have gained prominence in recent years due to their ability to handle complex tasks such as image recognition, natural language processing, and game playing.

Deep learning, a subfield of machine learning, focuses on neural networks with multiple hidden layers. These deep neural networks have demonstrated remarkable success in tasks like image classification, object detection, and machine translation. The deep learning revolution has been driven by advances in hardware, such as Graphics Processing Units (GPUs), and the availability of large-scale datasets.

In addition to selecting the right algorithm and model architecture, hyperparameter tuning plays a crucial role in optimizing a machine learning model. Hyperparameters are parameters that are not learned from the data but are set before training begins. These include learning rates, batch sizes, and the number of hidden layers in a neural network. Grid search and random search are common techniques used to find the best combination of hyperparameters for a given task.

Another essential aspect of machine learning is feature engineering. Feature engineering involves selecting and creating relevant features from the raw data to enhance a model's performance. A well-designed set of features can make a significant difference in the model's ability to learn and make accurate predictions. Feature engineering requires domain knowledge and creativity.

In recent years, there has been a surge in the use of pre-trained models and transfer learning. Pre-trained models are neural networks that have been trained on large datasets for specific tasks, such as image classification or natural language understanding. These models can be fine-tuned on a smaller, task-specific dataset, saving significant time and resources.

Interpreting machine learning models and understanding their decision-making processes are crucial, especially in applications where transparency and accountability are paramount. Techniques like feature importance analysis, gradient-based saliency maps, and SHAP (SHapley Additive exPlanations) values can provide insights into how a model arrives at its predictions.

Ethical considerations are also essential in the field of machine learning. Bias in data and algorithms can lead to unfair and discriminatory outcomes. It is crucial to assess and mitigate bias in both the data used for training and the models themselves. Fairness, accountability, and transparency should be integral parts of the machine learning development process.

The deployment of machine learning models into real-world applications is the ultimate goal. This involves integrating the trained model into a production environment where it can make predictions or decisions in real-time. Challenges such as model versioning, scalability, and monitoring for model drift must be addressed to ensure that the deployed model continues to perform well over time.

In summary, understanding the basics of machine learning is essential for anyone looking to work with this transformative technology. It involves data collection, preprocessing, algorithm selection, training, evaluation, and deployment. The choice of algorithm, model architecture, hyperparameters, and feature engineering all play a crucial role in the success of a machine learning project. Additionally, ethical considerations, transparency, and accountability should guide the development and deployment of machine learning models to ensure their responsible and fair use in society.

Deep learning is a subfield of machine learning that focuses on artificial neural networks, inspired by the structure and function of the human brain. It has gained significant attention and popularity in recent years due to its remarkable capabilities in various applications. Deep learning models are designed to automatically learn and represent data through a hierarchical approach, where each layer of neurons learns to capture increasingly abstract features from the input data.

At its core, deep learning is all about neural networks with multiple hidden layers, often referred to as deep neural networks. These networks can handle complex tasks and learn intricate patterns from vast amounts of data. The term "deep" in deep learning emphasizes the depth of these networks, which can have numerous hidden layers, making them capable of modeling highly complex relationships in data.

Deep learning models are particularly adept at tasks such as image and speech recognition, natural language processing, and playing strategic games like chess and Go. One of the reasons for their success is their ability to automatically discover relevant features from the raw data, reducing the need for manual feature engineering.

Deep learning has its roots in the field of artificial neural networks, which dates back to the 1940s and 1950s. However, it wasn't until the 2000s that deep learning gained widespread attention and started to show its true potential. The availability of large-scale datasets, increased computing power, and advancements in training algorithms played a pivotal role in the resurgence of deep learning.

A fundamental component of deep learning is the artificial neuron, which is inspired by the biological neuron found in the human brain. These artificial neurons, also known as nodes or units, are organized into layers within a neural network. The input layer receives the raw data, while the hidden layers progressively transform and abstract the information. The output layer produces the final prediction or decision based on the learned features.

Each connection between neurons in adjacent layers is associated with a weight, which determines the strength of the connection. During training, the neural network adjusts these weights through a process called backpropagation, which minimizes a specific loss function by iteratively updating the weights to reduce prediction errors. This training process allows the network to learn from labeled data and improve its performance.

Convolutional Neural Networks (CNNs) are a specific type of deep neural network commonly used for tasks related to computer vision, such as image classification and object detection. CNNs are designed to handle grid-like data, making them highly effective in capturing spatial patterns in images. They employ convolutional layers and pooling layers to automatically learn and extract relevant features from images.

Recurrent Neural Networks (RNNs) are another class of deep neural networks used for sequential data, such as time series and natural language processing. RNNs have connections that loop back on themselves, allowing them to maintain hidden states and capture temporal dependencies in data. This makes them suitable for tasks like text generation, language translation, and speech recognition.

The success of deep learning is closely tied to the availability of massive datasets, which provide ample examples for training deep neural networks. In addition to large datasets, deep learning models benefit from increased computational power, often using Graphics Processing Units (GPUs) to accelerate training. These advancements in hardware have enabled the training of deep networks with millions of parameters.

Transfer learning is a technique that has further propelled the capabilities of deep learning. With transfer learning, pre-trained models, which have been trained on vast datasets for specific tasks, can be fine-tuned on smaller, task-specific datasets. This approach significantly reduces the amount of data and time required to develop effective deep learning models for various applications.

Despite its success, deep learning is not without challenges. It can be data-hungry, meaning it often requires substantial amounts of labeled data for training. Overfitting, where a model performs well on the training data but poorly on unseen data, is also a common issue. Researchers and practitioners continually work on developing techniques to mitigate these challenges.

The field of deep learning is continually evolving, with ongoing research and development aimed at improving model performance, reducing data requirements, and making deep learning more interpretable and understandable. Ethical considerations, such as fairness and bias in deep learning models, are also crucial areas of focus to ensure responsible and equitable use of this technology.

In summary, deep learning is a subfield of machine learning that leverages artificial neural networks with multiple hidden layers to automatically learn and represent data. These deep neural networks have demonstrated remarkable capabilities in various applications, driven by advancements in data availability, computational power, and training algorithms. Convolutional Neural Networks and Recurrent Neural Networks are specialized architectures within deep learning, tailored for specific types of data. Transfer learning has further accelerated the adoption of deep learning, allowing pre-trained models to be fine-tuned for various tasks. While challenges exist, ongoing research and development continue to push the boundaries of what deep learning can achieve and contribute to its rapid evolution in the field of artificial intelligence.

Chapter 2: Understanding Neural Networks

Neurons and activation functions are fundamental components of artificial neural networks, forming the building blocks of deep learning models. These components play a crucial role in processing and transforming information within a neural network. Neurons are inspired by biological neurons found in the human brain, which transmit signals and process information through electrical and chemical signals. In artificial neural networks, neurons are mathematical units that receive input, perform computations, and produce output.

Each neuron in a neural network takes multiple input values, processes them using weighted connections, and produces an output value. The weighted connections represent the strength of the influence of each input on the neuron's output. These weights are learned during the training process and are adjusted to optimize the network's performance on a specific task.

The output of a neuron is determined by an activation function, which is a mathematical function that introduces non-linearity into the network. Activation functions are essential because they allow neural networks to model complex relationships and capture non-linear patterns in data. Without activation functions, neural networks would reduce to linear transformations, limiting their expressive power.

One of the most commonly used activation functions is the sigmoid function. The sigmoid function maps the weighted sum of inputs to a value between 0 and 1, making it suitable for binary classification problems where the output represents the probability of a certain class. However, sigmoid functions suffer from the vanishing gradient problem, which can slow down training in deep networks.

To address the vanishing gradient problem, the rectified linear unit (ReLU) activation function was introduced. ReLU is defined as the maximum of zero and the weighted sum of inputs. ReLU is computationally efficient and allows the network to learn faster and capture complex patterns. However, ReLU has its own challenges, such as the "dying ReLU" problem, where neurons can become inactive during training.

Leaky ReLU is a variant of the ReLU activation function that addresses the dying ReLU problem by allowing a small, non-zero gradient for negative input values. This ensures that even neurons that have learned poorly still contribute to the training process.

Another activation function called the hyperbolic tangent (tanh) function is similar to the sigmoid function but maps inputs to values between -1 and 1. Tanh is often used in recurrent neural networks (RNNs) and can be advantageous when data is centered around zero.

Recently, advanced activation functions like the Swish function and the Gated Linear Unit (GLU) have gained attention for their potential to improve model performance in specific scenarios. Swish is a smooth, non-monotonic function that has shown promising results in deep neural networks. GLU is commonly used in natural language processing tasks, as it enables models to capture long-range dependencies.

Choosing the right activation function for a neural network depends on the nature of the task and the characteristics of the data. Experimentation and hyperparameter tuning are often necessary to determine which activation function works best for a specific problem.

In addition to these common activation functions, there are other specialized functions like the softmax function, which is used in the output layer of neural networks for multi-class classification problems. The softmax function converts a vector of raw scores into a probability distribution over multiple classes.

In summary, neurons and activation functions are essential components of artificial neural networks. Neurons process input data through weighted connections, and activation functions introduce non-linearity into the network, allowing it to model complex relationships in data. Sigmoid, ReLU, Leaky ReLU, tanh, and other specialized activation functions each have their advantages and are chosen based on the specific requirements of a neural network and the problem it aims to solve. The selection of the right activation function is a crucial decision in designing effective neural networks.

Neural networks are a diverse family of machine learning models that have been developed to solve various types of tasks and problems. The choice of neural network architecture depends on the nature of the data and the specific problem you are trying to address. Here, we will explore some of the most common types of neural networks and their applications.

Feedforward Neural Networks (FNNs) are the simplest type of neural network, consisting of an input layer, one or more hidden layers, and an output layer. These networks are primarily used for supervised learning tasks such as regression and classification. They are called "feedforward" because the information flows in one direction, from the input layer to the output layer, without loops or feedback.

Convolutional Neural Networks (CNNs) are specialized neural networks designed for processing grid-like data, such as images and video. They employ convolutional layers that apply filters or kernels to local regions of the input, allowing them to capture spatial patterns and hierarchical features. CNNs are widely used in image classification, object detection, and image generation tasks.

Recurrent Neural Networks (RNNs) are designed to handle sequential data, making them suitable for tasks such as natural language processing and time series analysis. RNNs have connections that loop back on themselves, allowing them to maintain hidden states and capture temporal dependencies in data. However, they may suffer from vanishing or exploding gradient problems during training.

Long Short-Term Memory (LSTM) networks are a type of RNN that addresses the vanishing gradient problem. LSTMs have specialized memory cells and gating mechanisms that enable them to capture long-range dependencies in sequential data. They are widely used in applications like speech recognition and language translation.

Gated Recurrent Unit (GRU) networks are similar to LSTMs but have a simpler architecture with fewer gates. GRUs have been shown to perform well in various sequential data tasks and are computationally more efficient than LSTMs.

Autoencoders are a type of neural network used for unsupervised learning and dimensionality reduction. They consist of an encoder that maps input data to a lower-dimensional representation and a decoder that reconstructs the original data from the encoded representation. Autoencoders are often used for feature learning and data denoising.

Generative Adversarial Networks (GANs) consist of two neural networks: a generator and a discriminator. The generator aims to create data that is indistinguishable from real data, while the discriminator tries to distinguish between real and generated data. GANs are used for image generation, style transfer, and data augmentation.

Variational Autoencoders (VAEs) combine the concepts of autoencoders and probabilistic modeling. VAEs learn a probabilistic distribution over the encoded representations, enabling them to generate new data samples. They are often used for generative modeling and data generation tasks.

Siamese Networks are designed for tasks involving similarity or dissimilarity measures between pairs of data points. These networks consist of two identical subnetworks that share weights. Siamese networks are commonly used in face recognition, signature verification, and similarity-based recommendation systems.

Self-Organizing Maps (SOMs) are a type of unsupervised neural network used for clustering and visualization. SOMs learn to map high-dimensional input data onto a lower-dimensional grid of neurons, preserving the topological relationships between data points. They are often used for exploratory data analysis and feature visualization.

Radial Basis Function (RBF) Networks are a type of feedforward neural network with a unique architecture. They use radial basis functions as activation functions in the hidden layer and are used for tasks like function approximation and classification.

Modular Neural Networks consist of multiple neural networks or modules that work together to solve a complex task. Each module specializes in a specific subtask, and their outputs are combined to produce the final result. Modular neural networks are used in robotics, reinforcement learning, and multi-modal tasks.

Capsule Networks (CapsNets) are a recent advancement in neural network architecture designed to improve the handling of hierarchical and spatial relationships in data. CapsNets use capsules as fundamental units that capture features and pose information. They have shown promise in tasks like image segmentation and object recognition.

In the rapidly evolving field of deep learning, researchers continue to develop new types of neural networks and architectures tailored to specific challenges and domains. The choice of the right neural network for a given task is a critical decision that impacts the model's performance and efficiency. Understanding the strengths and weaknesses of different neural network types is essential for effectively applying deep learning to various applications and advancing the field further.

Chapter 3: Getting Started with Python and TensorFlow

Setting up your Python environment is a crucial first step in any data science or machine learning journey. A well-configured environment ensures that you have access to the necessary libraries, tools, and resources to work efficiently. Next, we will guide you through the process of setting up your Python environment.

Before you begin, it's essential to understand that Python has a vibrant and diverse ecosystem of libraries and packages that cater to different needs. One of the most popular Python distributions for data science and machine learning is Anaconda. Anaconda provides a comprehensive package manager called conda, which simplifies the installation and management of Python libraries and environments.

To get started, you'll need to download and install Anaconda from the official website, making sure to choose the version that matches your operating system. Once Anaconda is installed, you can open the Anaconda Navigator, a graphical user interface that allows you to manage environments and packages effortlessly. You can also use the Anaconda prompt or terminal to work with conda through the command line.

Creating a dedicated environment for your project is a best practice to avoid conflicts between libraries and dependencies. You can create a new environment using the conda command, specifying the Python version and any packages you want to install. For example, to create an environment called "myenv" with Python 3.7 and install the popular data science libraries NumPy and pandas, you can use the following command:

luaCopy code

```
conda create --name myenv python=3.7 numpy pandas
```
After creating the environment, you can activate it by running:

Copy code

```
conda activate myenv
```

This ensures that any Python-related commands you execute will use the packages installed in the "myenv" environment. You can deactivate the environment with the command:

Copy code

```
conda deactivate
```

Now that you have your environment set up, it's essential to install essential libraries for data manipulation, analysis, and visualization. Some of the most commonly used libraries include NumPy, pandas, Matplotlib, and Seaborn. You can install these libraries using conda or pip, another popular Python package manager.

For example, to install NumPy and pandas, you can use conda with the following commands:

Copy code

```
conda install numpy conda install pandas
```

Alternatively, you can use pip for installation:

Copy code

```
pip install numpy pip install pandas
```

It's worth noting that some libraries may have dependencies on system-level packages or external tools. For instance, libraries like OpenCV or TensorFlow may require additional installations and configurations. Always refer to the official documentation for each library to ensure you meet all the requirements.

To work efficiently with Python, especially in data science and machine learning, using an integrated development environment (IDE) can be immensely helpful. Popular Python IDEs include PyCharm, Visual Studio Code, and Jupyter

Notebook. Each IDE has its strengths, so you can choose the one that best suits your needs and preferences.

Jupyter Notebook, in particular, is an excellent choice for data exploration, analysis, and documentation. It allows you to create interactive notebooks that combine code, visualizations, and explanatory text. You can install Jupyter Notebook within your environment using conda or pip:

Copy code

```
conda install jupyter
```

Copy code

```
pip install jupyter
```

After installation, you can launch Jupyter Notebook by running:

Copy code

```
jupyter notebook
```

This will open a web-based interface where you can create new notebooks or open existing ones. Jupyter Notebook provides an excellent environment for experimenting with code, visualizing data, and documenting your work.

As you work with data and machine learning, you may also need to install specialized libraries such as scikit-learn, TensorFlow, or PyTorch. These libraries offer powerful tools for tasks like machine learning, deep learning, and neural network modeling. You can install them using conda or pip, following the installation instructions provided in their documentation.

In addition to libraries, you may find it useful to work with data in various formats, such as CSV, Excel, JSON, or databases. Python provides libraries like pandas and SQLAlchemy to handle these data formats and interact with databases.

For example, to read and write CSV files using pandas, you can use the following code:

```
pythonCopy code
import pandas as pd # Read a CSV file into a DataFrame
data = pd.read_csv('data.csv') # Write a DataFrame to a CSV
file data.to_csv('new_data.csv', index=False)
```

If you need to access databases, you can use SQLAlchemy, which supports various database management systems. You can install SQLAlchemy with conda or pip and then use it to connect to databases, query data, and perform database operations programmatically.

Setting up your Python environment is a crucial foundation for your data science and machine learning projects. A well-organized environment ensures that you have access to the necessary tools, libraries, and resources to work effectively. By following the steps outlined Next, you can create a dedicated environment, install essential libraries, choose an IDE, and handle data in various formats, setting you on the right path to tackle data-driven challenges and explore the exciting world of Python.

TensorFlow is an open-source machine learning framework developed by the Google Brain team, designed to make it easier to build and train deep neural networks. It has gained widespread popularity in both the research and industry communities due to its flexibility, scalability, and extensive ecosystem of tools and libraries. Next, we'll provide an introduction to TensorFlow, explore its key features, and discuss how to get started with this powerful framework.

TensorFlow is built around the concept of tensors, which are multi-dimensional arrays or data structures. These tensors flow through computational graphs, where nodes represent mathematical operations and edges represent the flow of data between nodes. This symbolic approach to computation allows for automatic differentiation, making it ideal for training complex machine learning models.

One of the core features of TensorFlow is its support for automatic differentiation, which is essential for training neural networks through techniques like backpropagation. By automatically calculating gradients, TensorFlow simplifies the process of optimizing model parameters using gradient-based optimization algorithms. This feature significantly accelerates the development of machine learning models.

TensorFlow provides a high-level, user-friendly API called Keras, which simplifies the construction and training of neural networks. Keras is now tightly integrated into TensorFlow, making it the default high-level API for building deep learning models. With Keras, you can quickly define neural network architectures using simple and intuitive code.

TensorFlow offers flexibility in terms of deployment, allowing you to run models on various platforms, including CPUs, GPUs, and TPUs (Tensor Processing Units). This versatility is crucial for scaling up the training of large models or deploying them in production environments. You can also deploy TensorFlow models to mobile devices and the web using TensorFlow Lite and TensorFlow.js, respectively.

The TensorFlow ecosystem includes various tools and libraries that facilitate model development, training, and deployment. TensorBoard, for example, is a visualization tool that helps you monitor training progress and visualize the structure of your neural networks. TensorFlow Extended (TFX) provides a comprehensive platform for deploying production-ready machine learning pipelines.

TensorFlow's support for distributed computing enables you to train large models across multiple machines or devices, which is crucial for tackling complex tasks such as deep reinforcement learning or natural language processing. The TensorFlow Serving framework simplifies the deployment of trained models in production environments, allowing for seamless integration with web services and applications.

To get started with TensorFlow, you'll need to install the framework, which can be done using pip. It's recommended to create a virtual environment for your TensorFlow projects to manage dependencies and avoid conflicts. Once TensorFlow is installed, you can import it into your Python scripts and begin building and training models.

TensorFlow provides a wide range of pre-built layers, optimizers, and loss functions, making it easier to construct and train neural networks. You can also create custom layers and loss functions to tailor your models to specific tasks. This flexibility allows you to experiment with different network architectures and fine-tune models according to your needs.

In TensorFlow, data is typically represented as tensors, and you can load and preprocess data using libraries like NumPy or TensorFlow Data Input (TF.data). Data pipelines in TensorFlow are efficient and can handle large datasets, making it suitable for tasks that require working with extensive data.

Once you have your data and model ready, you can compile the model using Keras and specify the optimizer, loss function, and evaluation metrics. This step prepares the model for training, and you can then use the fit() method to train the model on your training data.

TensorFlow provides a range of callback functions that allow you to monitor training progress, save model checkpoints, and implement early stopping. These callbacks are essential for fine-tuning hyperparameters and ensuring that your models converge effectively.

TensorFlow also supports transfer learning, allowing you to leverage pre-trained models and fine-tune them on specific tasks. This approach is especially useful when working with limited labeled data or when building models for image classification, object detection, and natural language understanding.

For example, you can use pre-trained models from the TensorFlow Hub or the TensorFlow Model Garden, which provides a collection of state-of-the-art models for various domains. Fine-tuning these models on your data can save significant time and resources.

TensorFlow's flexibility extends to its support for custom training loops, which provide fine-grained control over the training process. With custom training loops, you can implement advanced training techniques, such as curriculum learning, adversarial training, and reinforcement learning.

As you advance in your journey with TensorFlow, you'll find that the framework offers a wide array of resources, including documentation, tutorials, and community forums. The TensorFlow website and TensorFlow's official GitHub repository are valuable sources of information and code examples. You can also explore TensorFlow's YouTube channel, which features video tutorials and lectures on various machine learning topics.

In summary, TensorFlow is a versatile and powerful machine learning framework that has revolutionized the field of deep learning. With its support for automatic differentiation, high-level APIs like Keras, and an extensive ecosystem of tools and libraries, TensorFlow simplifies the development, training, and deployment of deep neural networks. Whether you're a beginner or an experienced machine learning practitioner, TensorFlow provides the tools and resources you need to tackle a wide range of tasks and challenges in the exciting world of artificial intelligence.

Chapter 4: Data Preprocessing for Deep Learning

Data cleaning and transformation are essential steps in the data preprocessing pipeline, ensuring that the data you work with is accurate, consistent, and suitable for analysis or modeling purposes. Cleaning and transforming data can be a time-consuming process, but it is a critical one for obtaining reliable and meaningful insights from your datasets. Next, we will delve into the importance of data cleaning and transformation, explore common data issues, and provide techniques to address them effectively.

The first step in the data cleaning process is data inspection, where you thoroughly examine your dataset to identify any anomalies or issues. This includes checking for missing values, outliers, inconsistencies, and duplicate records. By understanding the quality and characteristics of your data, you can make informed decisions on how to proceed with cleaning and transformation.

Missing data is a common issue in datasets and can occur for various reasons, such as data entry errors or incomplete records. Handling missing data is essential because it can lead to biased or inaccurate results if not addressed properly. Techniques for dealing with missing data include imputation, where missing values are replaced with estimated values, or removal of rows or columns with excessive missing data.

Outliers, or extreme values that deviate significantly from the rest of the data, can distort statistical analyses and machine learning models. Detecting outliers often involves visualizing data using techniques like box plots or scatter plots and applying statistical tests or methods such as the Z-score or the Interquartile Range (IQR). Outliers can be treated through techniques such as transformation, capping, or removing them, depending on the context and goals of the analysis.

Inconsistent or erroneous data entries, such as typos or inconsistent formats, can hinder data analysis and interpretation. Data consistency checks and standardization techniques, such as converting text to lowercase, can help address these issues. Data standardization ensures that data is in a consistent format, making it easier to work with and analyze.

Duplicate records in a dataset can lead to redundancy and bias in analyses, as well as wasting computational resources. Identifying and removing duplicate records is a crucial step in data cleaning. Common methods for detecting duplicates involve comparing entire rows or specific columns and removing or consolidating identical or highly similar records.

Once you've addressed missing values, outliers, and inconsistencies, you can move on to data transformation, which involves reshaping and reorganizing the data to make it suitable for analysis or modeling. Data transformation can include tasks such as encoding categorical variables, scaling numerical features, and creating new features or aggregates. Categorical variables, which represent categories or groups, often need to be encoded into numerical values for machine learning algorithms. Common encoding techniques include one-hot encoding, where each category becomes a binary column, or label encoding, where categories are mapped to integers. Choosing the appropriate encoding method depends on the nature of the categorical variable and the specific modeling task.

Numerical feature scaling is essential when working with algorithms that are sensitive to the magnitude of variables, such as gradient-based optimization methods. Common scaling techniques include standardization (z-score normalization) and min-max scaling, which transform numerical features to have a specified range or mean and standard deviation.

Feature engineering is a critical aspect of data transformation, as it involves creating new features or aggregating existing ones to improve the performance of machine learning models. Feature engineering can include tasks such as extracting date-related features from timestamps, creating interaction terms between variables, or deriving statistical measures like means or medians. Effective feature engineering requires domain knowledge and an understanding of the problem you are trying to solve.

Data transformation also encompasses the handling of imbalanced datasets, where one class or category is significantly underrepresented. Techniques like oversampling, undersampling, or synthetic data generation can address class imbalance and improve model performance. These methods aim to create a more balanced training dataset for machine learning algorithms.

Data cleaning and transformation are iterative processes that require constant validation and testing to ensure that the resulting dataset is appropriate for analysis or modeling. It is essential to document all cleaning and transformation steps thoroughly to maintain transparency and reproducibility. Data cleaning and transformation are often performed in conjunction with exploratory data analysis (EDA) to gain insights into the dataset's characteristics and better understand the data.

Tools and libraries such as Python's pandas, NumPy, and scikit-learn provide a wide range of functions and methods to assist with data cleaning and transformation. These libraries offer efficient ways to manipulate and preprocess data, making the process more manageable and less error-prone.

In summary, data cleaning and transformation are fundamental steps in the data preprocessing pipeline, ensuring that data is accurate, consistent, and suitable for analysis or modeling. Addressing issues like missing values, outliers, inconsistencies, and duplicates is crucial to obtaining reliable insights from your datasets. Data transformation involves encoding categorical variables, scaling numerical features, and performing feature engineering to improve model performance. By following best practices and using appropriate tools, you can prepare your data for analysis and maximize the effectiveness of your data-driven projects.

Data augmentation is a vital technique in the realm of computer vision, natural language processing, and other machine learning domains where data is a critical component. Data augmentation involves creating new training examples by applying various transformations to the existing data. The goal is to increase the diversity of the training dataset, which can improve the model's generalization, robustness, and performance on unseen data.

In computer vision, data augmentation techniques are particularly valuable because they can enhance the model's ability to recognize objects, patterns, and features under different conditions. One of the simplest and most commonly used data augmentation techniques for images is random cropping. This involves selecting a random region of the input image and resizing it to the desired dimensions. Random cropping helps the model learn to recognize objects from various positions and scales, making it more robust to variations in object placement within images.

Another powerful technique is horizontal flipping, where an image is horizontally mirrored. This simple transformation can effectively double the size of the training dataset while maintaining label consistency. Horizontal flipping is especially useful for tasks where object orientation does not affect the desired outcome, such as image classification.

Rotation is another data augmentation technique that introduces diversity into the dataset. By randomly rotating images by various degrees, the model learns to recognize objects from different angles. Rotation augmentation can be particularly beneficial for tasks like object detection or image segmentation, where object orientation matters.

Adding noise to images is a common technique for improving a model's robustness to variations in lighting and pixel-level artifacts. Gaussian noise, salt-and-pepper noise, or speckle noise can be applied to images to simulate real-world imperfections. Noise augmentation helps the model generalize better to noisy or low-quality images.

Color jittering is a technique used to change the color distribution of images. By randomly adjusting brightness, contrast, saturation, and hue, color jittering can help the model become invariant to changes in lighting conditions. This is especially valuable for tasks like image classification where color variations should not affect the model's predictions.

In natural language processing, data augmentation techniques are designed to manipulate and generate new text data. One common technique is text augmentation, which involves synonym replacement, word deletion, or word insertion. Synonym replacement replaces words in a sentence with synonyms from a thesaurus, expanding the vocabulary of the training data. Word deletion randomly removes words from a sentence to create shorter variations. Word insertion introduces new words into a sentence to increase its length.

Back-translation is a powerful technique used for generating parallel data, commonly applied to machine translation tasks. It involves translating a sentence from the source language to the target language and then translating it back to the source language. This process introduces variations in the sentence structure and wording, effectively creating new training examples.

Data augmentation can be applied to audio data as well, especially in tasks like speech recognition or audio classification. Time stretching and pitch shifting are common techniques for audio data augmentation. Time stretching involves stretching or compressing the audio signal in time, which changes its duration. Pitch shifting modifies the pitch of the audio signal while preserving its tempo. These transformations can help the model generalize better to variations in speech speed and pitch.

In data augmentation, it's essential to strike a balance between introducing diversity and maintaining label consistency. Random transformations should not alter the meaning or semantics of the data, ensuring that the augmented examples are still relevant for training. For example, in text data augmentation, synonym replacement should not change the core meaning of the sentence.

Augmenting data in moderation can prevent overfitting, where the model memorizes the training data rather than learning general patterns. However, excessive augmentation may lead to over-regularization, where the model becomes too invariant to variations and loses the ability to capture subtle features in the data. The choice of augmentation techniques and their parameters should be carefully tuned to achieve the right balance.

Furthermore, it's crucial to consider the computational cost of data augmentation. Applying random transformations during training can significantly increase the computational requirements and training time. Therefore, it's essential to strike a balance between augmentation benefits and computational resources available.

Data augmentation is a versatile technique that can be customized to specific tasks and domains. In addition to the techniques mentioned above, domain-specific augmentations can be developed to address unique challenges. For example, in medical imaging, data augmentation techniques may focus on simulating variations in patient demographics, imaging equipment, or image quality.

In summary, data augmentation is a powerful technique used to improve the performance, generalization, and robustness of machine learning models. It involves applying various transformations to the training data, creating new examples that expose the model to different variations and conditions. Data augmentation is especially valuable in computer vision, natural language processing, and audio processing tasks, where diversity in the training data can lead to more robust and accurate models. However, careful consideration of label consistency, computational resources, and task-specific requirements is essential when applying data augmentation techniques effectively.

Chapter 5: Training Your First Neural Network

Building and compiling a neural network are fundamental steps in deep learning, as they define the architecture of the model and its training process. Next, we will explore the process of constructing a neural network, specifying its layers, and configuring the training settings. By understanding how to build and compile neural networks, you can create powerful models for various machine learning tasks.

The first step in building a neural network is defining its architecture, which involves specifying the number of layers, the type of layers, and their connections. Neural networks consist of layers arranged in a sequential manner, forming a computational graph. The first layer is typically the input layer, which receives the data, while the last layer is the output layer, providing the model's predictions.

In between the input and output layers, you can add one or more hidden layers that perform transformations and feature extractions. These hidden layers can be dense (fully connected), convolutional, recurrent, or any other type of layer suitable for the task at hand. The choice of layer types and their architecture depends on the specific problem you are trying to solve.

For example, in image classification tasks, convolutional layers are commonly used to capture spatial patterns, while recurrent layers are employed for sequence data like natural language text. Dense layers, also known as fully connected layers, are versatile and can be used for various tasks, including regression and classification.

To build a neural network in popular deep learning frameworks like TensorFlow or Keras, you typically start by initializing a sequential model or a similar container. Then, you add layers to the model one by one using simple commands.

Each layer is configured with specific parameters, such as the number of units or neurons, activation functions, and input shapes. For example, to create a simple feedforward neural network with three layers in Keras, you can use the following code:

pythonCopy code

```
from tensorflow import keras model = keras.Sequential([
keras.layers.Dense(64, activation='relu',
input_shape=(input_dim,)), keras.layers.Dense(32,
activation='relu'), keras.layers.Dense(output_dim,
activation='softmax') ])
```

In this example, we define a sequential model and add three dense layers with the specified number of units and activation functions. The input shape is specified only for the first layer, as subsequent layers can infer their input shapes automatically.

Once you have built the architecture of your neural network, the next step is to compile it by configuring the training process. To compile a neural network, you need to specify three key components: the optimizer, the loss function, and the evaluation metrics.

The optimizer is responsible for updating the model's weights during training to minimize the loss. Common optimizers include stochastic gradient descent (SGD), Adam, RMSprop, and more. Each optimizer has its unique update rules and hyperparameters, and the choice depends on the specific problem and model architecture.

The loss function quantifies the difference between the predicted output and the true target values. The goal during training is to minimize this loss, effectively aligning the model's predictions with the desired outcomes. The choice of the loss function depends on the nature of the task; for example, mean squared error is commonly used for regression, while categorical cross-entropy is suitable for classification.

Evaluation metrics are used to monitor the model's performance during training and evaluation. These metrics provide additional insights into how well the model is performing beyond the loss value. Common evaluation metrics for classification tasks include accuracy, precision, recall, F1 score, and area under the receiver operating characteristic curve (AUC-ROC). For regression tasks, metrics like mean absolute error (MAE) and mean squared error (MSE) are commonly used.

To compile a neural network in Keras, you can use the following code:

pythonCopy code

```
model.compile(optimizer='adam',
loss='categorical_crossentropy', metrics=['accuracy'])
```

In this example, we specify the Adam optimizer, categorical cross-entropy loss for a classification task, and accuracy as the evaluation metric. These settings configure the training process and define how the model will update its weights during optimization.

Before training the model, it's essential to prepare the training data, validation data, and test data. Typically, the dataset is split into three sets: the training set, which is used for model training; the validation set, which is used for model tuning and early stopping; and the test set, which is used to evaluate the final model's performance.

Data preprocessing, including normalization, scaling, and encoding of categorical variables, may also be required before training. Proper data preparation ensures that the model can learn effectively from the training data and generalize well to unseen data.

To train the compiled neural network, you can use the **fit()** method in Keras. You provide the training data, specify the number of epochs (iterations over the dataset), batch size (number of samples used in each update), and validation data if available.

pythonCopy code

```
history = model.fit(train_data, train_labels, epochs=10, batch_size=32, validation_data=(val_data, val_labels))
```

The **fit()** method trains the model on the training data, updating the weights using the specified optimizer and minimizing the loss function. During training, you can monitor various metrics, such as training and validation loss and accuracy, to assess the model's performance and make adjustments if necessary.

After training, you can evaluate the model's performance on the test data to assess how well it generalizes to unseen examples. The **evaluate()** method in Keras provides the final performance metrics based on the test data.

pythonCopy code

```
test_loss, test_accuracy = model.evaluate(test_data, test_labels)
```

By building and compiling a neural network, you define the model's architecture and training process, preparing it for learning from the data. Understanding how to specify layers, compile the model with the right optimizer, loss function, and evaluation metrics, and train it on properly prepared data is essential for creating effective deep learning models for a wide range of machine learning tasks.

In summary, building and compiling a neural network are fundamental steps in the deep learning workflow. By defining the model's architecture and configuring the training process, you set the stage for effective learning from the data. Understanding how to add layers, choose optimizers, specify loss functions, and evaluate the model's performance is crucial for successfully creating and training deep neural networks for various machine learning tasks.

Training and evaluating a neural network is the heart of the machine learning process, where the model learns from the data and is tested for its ability to make accurate predictions. Next, we will dive into the intricacies of training neural networks, discussing topics like backpropagation, gradient descent, and overfitting. We will also explore techniques for evaluating and fine-tuning your models to ensure they perform well on real-world data.

Training a neural network involves optimizing its parameters, which are the weights and biases associated with the network's layers. The objective is to minimize a loss function that quantifies the difference between the model's predictions and the true target values. One of the most commonly used optimization algorithms for training neural networks is gradient descent.

Gradient descent is an iterative optimization algorithm that adjusts the model's parameters in the direction that reduces the loss. The key idea is to calculate the gradient of the loss function with respect to the parameters, which indicates how the loss would change if the parameters were adjusted slightly. By moving the parameters in the opposite direction of the gradient, the algorithm seeks to find the minimum of the loss function.

Backpropagation is a crucial technique for efficiently calculating gradients in neural networks. It involves propagating the error or loss backward through the network, layer by layer, to compute the gradients with respect to each parameter. The chain rule from calculus is applied to calculate these gradients efficiently. Backpropagation enables gradient descent to adjust the parameters effectively during training.

During training, the dataset is typically divided into mini-batches, and gradient descent is applied to each mini-batch rather than the entire dataset. This approach, known as mini-batch gradient descent, speeds up the training process and allows the model to update its parameters more frequently. The size of the mini-batch, known as the batch size, is a hyperparameter that affects the training process and should be tuned for each specific task.

Learning rate is another critical hyperparameter in gradient descent. It determines the size of the steps taken during parameter updates. A large learning rate can cause the algorithm to converge quickly but risk overshooting the minimum, while a small learning rate may lead to slow convergence or getting stuck in local minima. Finding an appropriate learning rate is essential for efficient training.

To avoid the model learning from the noise in the data and overfitting, regularization techniques are often applied during training. L2 regularization, for example, adds a penalty term to the loss function that discourages large parameter values. This helps prevent the model from fitting the training data too closely and encourages it to generalize better to unseen data.

Dropout is another regularization technique that randomly drops a fraction of neurons during training. This prevents individual neurons from becoming overly reliant on specific features in the data, promoting better generalization. Dropout has been particularly effective in reducing overfitting in deep neural networks.

Training a neural network involves choosing the right number of training epochs, which are the number of times the model iterates through the entire training dataset. Too few epochs may result in underfitting, where the model fails to capture important patterns in the data. Conversely, too many epochs can lead to overfitting, where the model learns the training data too well and performs poorly on unseen data.

Early stopping is a technique used to mitigate overfitting by monitoring the model's performance on a validation dataset during training. If the validation performance starts to degrade, training is halted, preventing the model from continuing to overfit. This technique ensures that the model is stopped at the point of optimal generalization.

Once a neural network is trained, it's essential to evaluate its performance on unseen data to assess its real-world utility. The test dataset, which was not used during training, is used for this purpose. Evaluating a model involves calculating various metrics, depending on the task.

In classification tasks, metrics like accuracy, precision, recall, F1 score, and the receiver operating characteristic (ROC) curve are commonly used. These metrics assess the model's ability to classify data correctly and distinguish between different classes.

In regression tasks, metrics such as mean absolute error (MAE), mean squared error (MSE), and root mean squared error (RMSE) measure the model's ability to predict numerical values accurately.

In natural language processing tasks, evaluation metrics may include accuracy, BLEU score for machine translation, or perplexity for language modeling.

The choice of evaluation metrics depends on the specific task and the desired performance criteria. For example, in medical diagnostics, achieving high sensitivity (recall) may be more important than overall accuracy.

To evaluate a model in practice, you can use the **evaluate()** method in deep learning frameworks like Keras. This method takes the test dataset as input and provides the chosen evaluation metrics as output.

pythonCopy code

```
test_loss, test_accuracy = model.evaluate(test_data, test_labels)
```

By assessing the model's performance on the test dataset, you gain insights into how well it generalizes to unseen data and whether it meets the desired performance criteria.

Fine-tuning a neural network is the process of making adjustments to improve its performance further. Fine-tuning may involve hyperparameter tuning, architectural changes, or additional data collection and augmentation.

Hyperparameter tuning explores different combinations of hyperparameters, such as learning rate, batch size, or the number of hidden layers. This process is often automated using techniques like grid search or random search to find the optimal set of hyperparameters that result in the best performance.

Architectural changes may involve modifying the neural network's architecture by adding or removing layers, adjusting the number of neurons, or trying different activation functions. These changes aim to find a better representation of the data and improve the model's performance.

Additional data collection and augmentation can also enhance a model's performance by providing more diverse and relevant training examples. Data augmentation techniques, as discussed earlier, can artificially increase the size and diversity of the training dataset, further improving the model's ability to generalize.

In summary, training and evaluating a neural network involve essential steps in the machine learning workflow. Training involves optimizing the model's parameters using gradient descent and backpropagation, with careful consideration of hyperparameters and regularization techniques. Evaluating the model's performance on a test dataset provides insights into its real-world utility and guides further improvements. Fine-tuning the model may be necessary to achieve the desired level of performance and generalization. By mastering these techniques, you can develop effective deep learning models for a wide range of tasks and domains.

Chapter 6: Convolutional Neural Networks (CNNs) Explained

Convolutional layers and filters are fundamental components of convolutional neural networks (CNNs), a class of deep learning models widely used for image and signal processing tasks. Next, we will delve into the architecture of convolutional layers, the concept of filters, and how they enable CNNs to learn hierarchical features from input data. Understanding convolutional layers and filters is essential for grasping the inner workings of CNNs and their impressive performance on various visual recognition tasks.

Convolutional layers play a pivotal role in CNNs, as they are responsible for capturing spatial patterns and features from input data. Unlike fully connected layers in traditional neural networks, convolutional layers employ a sliding window approach to process data. This approach allows them to learn local patterns and hierarchically build up representations of the input.

At the core of a convolutional layer are filters, also known as kernels. Filters are small, learnable weight matrices that slide over the input data to perform convolution operations. These operations involve element-wise multiplication of the filter with a local region of the input, followed by summation of the results to produce a single output value. The filter is then moved to the next position, and the process is repeated, creating an output feature map.

Filters serve as feature detectors, learning to recognize specific patterns or features in the input data. For example, in the early layers of a CNN, filters may learn to detect simple features like edges, corners, or textures. As we move deeper into the network, filters become more complex and start identifying higher-level features, such as shapes, object parts, or even entire objects.

The size of a filter, often referred to as the receptive field or kernel size, determines the spatial extent of the local region it processes. A common choice for filter sizes is 3x3 or 5x5, although larger and smaller sizes can be used depending on the task and architecture. Larger filters capture more extensive patterns, while smaller filters focus on finer details.

Convolutional layers apply multiple filters in parallel to the input data, resulting in multiple feature maps. These feature maps represent the presence of different features across the input. The number of filters used in a convolutional layer is a hyperparameter that affects the capacity and expressiveness of the network.

To calculate the output size of a feature map, the following formula is often used:

cssCopy code

```
output_size = (input_size - filter_size + 2 * padding) / stride
+ 1
```

Where:

input_size is the size of the input (e.g., width or height).

filter_size is the size of the filter (kernel).

padding is the amount of zero-padding applied to the input (if any).

stride is the step size at which the filter is moved across the input.

Padding and stride are additional hyperparameters that can be adjusted to control the size and behavior of the feature maps. Padding is used to preserve the spatial dimensions of the input, and it can be either "valid" (no padding) or "same" (pad to maintain size). Stride controls how much the filter moves between calculations, affecting the spatial resolution of the feature maps.

One of the advantages of convolutional layers is weight sharing. In a fully connected layer, each neuron has its set of weights, leading to a massive number of parameters in deep networks. Convolutional layers, on the other hand, share the same filter weights across different spatial positions of the input. This weight sharing reduces the number of parameters significantly, making CNNs more efficient and capable of learning from fewer training examples.

Stride affects the spatial resolution of the feature maps, as larger strides result in smaller output sizes. Reducing the spatial resolution can be useful in certain situations to decrease computational complexity or overfitting. However, it may also lead to a loss of spatial details.

Max-pooling and average-pooling are common techniques used to downsample feature maps and reduce their spatial dimensions further. Pooling layers apply a pooling operation (e.g., max or average) to non-overlapping regions of the feature map. This operation selects the maximum or average value within each region and produces a pooled feature map with reduced size.

The choice of pooling operation and pooling size are hyperparameters that can be adjusted based on the task. Pooling layers help the network focus on the most relevant features while discarding less informative spatial details. They also introduce a degree of translation invariance, as the presence of a feature in a slightly different position still leads to the same pooled output.

In modern CNN architectures, convolutional layers are often stacked multiple times to create deep networks. This deep hierarchy allows CNNs to learn increasingly abstract and complex features from the input data. Convolutional layers are typically followed by fully connected layers that perform classification or regression based on the extracted features.

Training a CNN involves optimizing the filter weights using backpropagation and gradient descent. During training, the network learns to recognize features that are relevant to the given task. Convolutional layers and filters, with their ability to capture hierarchical features, have proven highly effective in a wide range of applications, including image classification, object detection, image segmentation, and more.

In summary, convolutional layers and filters are foundational components of convolutional neural networks, enabling them to learn hierarchical features from input data. Filters serve as feature detectors, capturing patterns and structures at different levels of abstraction. Convolutional layers apply multiple filters to produce feature maps that represent the presence of these features. By stacking convolutional layers and combining them with pooling and fully connected layers, CNNs can learn complex representations of data and achieve state-of-the-art performance in various visual recognition tasks.

CNN architectures have evolved significantly over the years, leading to the development of powerful models with widespread applications in computer vision and beyond. Next, we will explore some of the most influential CNN architectures and delve into their applications, highlighting their impact on various domains of artificial intelligence.

One of the pioneering CNN architectures is LeNet-5, designed by Yann LeCun in the early 1990s, primarily for handwritten digit recognition. LeNet-5 introduced the concept of convolutional layers and max-pooling layers, setting the stage for future CNNs. While it may seem modest by today's standards, LeNet-5 revolutionized the field of computer vision.

AlexNet, introduced by Alex Krizhevsky in 2012, marked a significant breakthrough in image classification. This deep CNN architecture won the ImageNet Large Scale Visual Recognition Challenge (ILSVRC) by a wide margin, showcasing the potential of deep learning. AlexNet incorporated multiple convolutional layers and employed rectified linear unit (ReLU) activation functions, which accelerated training.

VGGNet, proposed by the Visual Geometry Group at the University of Oxford in 2014, emphasized network depth. VGGNet architectures had a uniform structure with a fixed 3x3 convolutional kernel size and a focus on stacking multiple layers. VGG16 and VGG19, with 16 and 19 weight layers, respectively, became popular choices for various image analysis tasks.

GoogLeNet, or Inception, introduced the concept of inception modules in 2014, developed by researchers at Google. These modules contained multiple convolutional filters with varying kernel sizes, enabling the network to capture features at different scales. GoogLeNet was not only accurate but also computationally efficient, leading to its adoption in various applications.

ResNet, short for Residual Network, proposed by Kaiming He et al. in 2015, addressed the challenge of training very deep networks. ResNet introduced residual connections that allowed gradients to flow more efficiently during training. This architectural innovation led to the creation of extremely deep networks with thousands of layers, achieving state-of-the-art results in image classification.

The success of CNN architectures extended beyond image classification to tasks like object detection. Faster R-CNN, introduced in 2015, combined the power of CNNs with region proposal networks (RPNs) to achieve real-time object detection. This architecture revolutionized object detection by significantly improving accuracy and speed.

CNNs have also been applied to the task of image segmentation, where the goal is to classify each pixel in an image into a specific category. U-Net, proposed by Olaf Ronneberger et al. in 2015, introduced a novel architecture with skip connections. These connections enabled U-Net to produce highly accurate pixel-wise predictions and became a cornerstone in medical image segmentation.

In the domain of natural language processing, CNNs have been adapted for text-based tasks. The use of 1D convolutions with text sequences, followed by max-pooling or global pooling, allows CNNs to capture local patterns in text data. This approach has been successful in tasks such as text classification and sentiment analysis.

CNN architectures have also found applications in the field of autonomous driving. Models like the convolutional neural network (CNN) for end-to-end autonomous driving, introduced by NVIDIA in 2016, have shown promising results in self-driving car applications. These models can learn to control a vehicle directly from raw sensor inputs, such as camera images, steering angles, and speed.

Medical imaging has been transformed by CNNs, with applications ranging from disease diagnosis to image-based interventions. Deep learning models have demonstrated exceptional accuracy in tasks such as detecting tumors in radiology images and segmenting structures in medical scans.

CNN architectures have even been employed in the creation of generative models. Generative Adversarial Networks (GANs), including DCGAN (Deep Convolutional GAN) and StyleGAN, leverage convolutional layers to generate realistic images. These models have been used in art generation, image-to-image translation, and data augmentation.

In the field of computer vision, transfer learning with pre-trained CNNs has become a common practice. Researchers and practitioners often fine-tune existing CNN architectures on new tasks, leveraging the knowledge acquired during pre-training. This approach reduces the need for extensive labeled data and accelerates model development.

The impact of CNN architectures extends to various applications in robotics. CNNs are used in robot perception tasks, enabling robots to recognize objects, navigate environments, and perform tasks like grasping and manipulation. CNN-based models have made significant contributions to the field of autonomous robots and human-robot interaction.

The applications of CNN architectures are not limited to vision-based tasks. They have been adapted for audio processing, such as speech recognition and environmental sound classification. CNNs can analyze spectrograms and other audio representations, making them valuable tools in audio-related applications.

In the financial sector, CNNs have been applied to time-series data for tasks like stock price prediction and anomaly detection. These models can capture temporal patterns and trends in financial data, assisting in decision-making and risk management.

Furthermore, CNN architectures have been employed in the domain of remote sensing. Satellite and aerial imagery analysis benefit from CNNs, which can classify land cover, detect changes, and identify objects of interest. These applications have implications for agriculture, environmental monitoring, and disaster management.

In summary, CNN architectures have played a transformative role in artificial intelligence, particularly in computer vision.

From LeNet-5 to ResNet and beyond, these architectures have continuously pushed the boundaries of what is possible in image analysis. Their applications span a wide range of domains, from medical imaging and autonomous driving to natural language processing and robotics. As CNN architectures continue to evolve, they will likely unlock new possibilities and advance the field of AI even further.

Chapter 7: Recurrent Neural Networks (RNNs) and Sequence Learning

Recurrent Neural Networks (RNNs) are a class of artificial neural networks specially designed to handle sequential data. Next, we will explore the fundamentals of RNNs, their architecture, and their applications across a wide range of domains. Understanding RNNs is essential for tackling tasks involving time series, natural language processing, speech recognition, and more.

RNNs are well-suited for sequential data because they maintain a hidden state or memory that can capture information from previous time steps. This memory allows RNNs to process sequences of variable length and learn patterns and dependencies within the data.

At the core of an RNN is a recurrent unit, which processes input data and updates the hidden state at each time step. The hidden state serves as a form of memory that retains information about previous time steps, making it accessible to the network for future predictions. This ability to maintain context over time is a key feature that distinguishes RNNs from other neural network architectures.

The architecture of an RNN typically consists of an input layer, one or more recurrent layers, and an output layer. The input layer receives the sequential data at each time step, while the recurrent layers process the data and update the hidden state. The output layer produces predictions or classifications based on the hidden state's information.

Mathematically, the computation within an RNN can be described as follows:

Input data at each time step is combined with the previous hidden state to produce a new hidden state.

The new hidden state becomes the input to the next time step, allowing information to flow through the sequence.

The output layer can produce predictions at each time step, or it can produce a single output at the end of the sequence, depending on the task.

One limitation of traditional RNNs is the vanishing gradient problem, which arises during training. As information flows through the network over multiple time steps, gradients can become very small, causing the network to have difficulty learning long-range dependencies. To address this issue, various RNN variants have been introduced.

Long Short-Term Memory (LSTM) networks, proposed by Sepp Hochreiter and Jürgen Schmidhuber in 1997, are a type of RNN that mitigates the vanishing gradient problem. LSTMs introduce a gating mechanism that allows the network to learn when to update and forget information in the hidden state. This gating mechanism provides better control over the flow of information, enabling LSTMs to capture long-range dependencies in sequential data effectively.

Another RNN variant, known as Gated Recurrent Unit (GRU), was introduced by Cho et al. in 2014. GRUs offer a similar solution to the vanishing gradient problem as LSTMs but with a simpler architecture. They use gating mechanisms to control the flow of information in the hidden state, making them computationally more efficient.

RNNs and their variants have found applications in a wide range of domains. In natural language processing (NLP), RNNs are used for tasks such as language modeling, text generation, and machine translation. They can process sequences of words or characters, capturing the context and semantics of language.

Speech recognition systems leverage RNNs to transcribe spoken language into text. By processing audio data as sequential inputs, RNNs can learn to recognize phonetic patterns and convert them into textual representations.

In time series forecasting, RNNs are applied to predict future values based on historical data. This is useful in domains like finance, where stock prices, exchange rates, and economic indicators are predicted.

RNNs have been instrumental in the field of robotics, enabling robots to navigate and interact with their environments. Recurrent networks can process sensor data over time, allowing robots to perceive and react to dynamic surroundings.

Healthcare benefits from RNNs in various applications, including patient monitoring, disease prediction, and medical image analysis. Sequential patient data can be used to predict health outcomes and recommend personalized treatments.

In autonomous vehicles, RNNs play a critical role in processing sensor data from cameras, LiDAR, and other sensors. These networks enable self-driving cars to perceive their surroundings, make decisions, and navigate safely.

RNNs have revolutionized the field of music generation and composition. By training on sequences of musical notes, RNNs can generate original compositions and harmonize with human musicians.

In the world of finance, RNNs are used for tasks such as predicting stock prices, analyzing market sentiment, and detecting financial fraud. Sequential financial data is well-suited to RNNs, which can uncover patterns and anomalies.

RNNs have also found applications in natural language understanding, where they are used to extract information and insights from unstructured text data. This includes tasks like sentiment analysis, entity recognition, and text summarization.

Despite their effectiveness, RNNs have certain limitations. They can be computationally expensive, making them less suitable for real-time applications. Training deep RNNs may require significant computational resources and time.

Furthermore, RNNs struggle with capturing extremely long-term dependencies in sequences. While LSTMs and GRUs mitigate the vanishing gradient problem, they may still have difficulty modeling very distant dependencies.

To address these limitations, attention mechanisms have been introduced. Attention mechanisms allow the network to focus on specific parts of the input sequence, giving more weight to relevant information. This enables RNNs to capture long-range dependencies more effectively and improves their performance on tasks like machine translation and document summarization.

In summary, Recurrent Neural Networks are a powerful class of neural networks designed to handle sequential data. Their ability to capture temporal dependencies has made them invaluable in a wide range of applications, from natural language processing and speech recognition to robotics and healthcare. While RNNs and their variants have addressed many challenges, ongoing research continues to push the boundaries of what can be achieved with sequential data analysis.

Sequence-to-Sequence (Seq2Seq) models represent a powerful class of neural networks that have demonstrated remarkable capabilities in handling sequential data. Next, we will delve into the architecture and applications of Seq2Seq models, which are designed to map sequences from one domain to another, making them invaluable in various natural language processing, machine translation, and sequence generation tasks.

The fundamental concept behind Seq2Seq models is the ability to take an input sequence of arbitrary length and produce an output sequence of potentially different length. This flexibility makes them suitable for tasks where the input and output sequences have a variable relationship, such as translation, summarization, and text generation.

At the heart of a Seq2Seq model is an encoder-decoder architecture. The encoder's role is to process the input sequence and transform it into a fixed-length context vector, which captures the essential information from the input. The decoder then takes this context vector and generates the output sequence step by step.

The encoder typically consists of recurrent layers, such as LSTM or GRU, which process the input sequence one element at a time while maintaining a hidden state. As the encoder processes each element, it updates the hidden state to capture the context of the input sequence. The final hidden state, which summarizes the entire input sequence, becomes the context vector that is passed to the decoder.

The decoder, also composed of recurrent layers, takes the context vector as an initial hidden state and generates the output sequence one element at a time. At each time step, the decoder predicts the next element in the output sequence based on the context vector and the previously generated elements. The generated element is then appended to the output sequence, and the process repeats until the desired length or an end-of-sequence token is reached.

Training a Seq2Seq model involves optimizing the model's parameters to minimize a loss function that quantifies the difference between the predicted and target sequences. Common loss functions for sequence generation tasks include cross-entropy loss and sequence-to-sequence loss, which account for the varying lengths of input and output sequences.

Seq2Seq models have gained significant popularity in machine translation tasks, where they have largely replaced traditional statistical machine translation models. In machine translation, the input is a sentence in one language, and the output is the corresponding sentence in another language. The encoder processes the source language sentence, and the decoder generates the target language sentence. This approach has led to substantial improvements in translation quality.

Seq2Seq models have also been applied to text summarization tasks, where the goal is to generate a concise summary of a longer document. The encoder processes the document, and the decoder generates a summary by selecting the most important information. This is achieved through techniques like attention mechanisms, which allow the model to focus on different parts of the input sequence while generating the output sequence.

In the realm of speech recognition, Seq2Seq models have made significant strides in converting spoken language into text. The input sequence consists of audio features or spectrograms, and the output sequence is the corresponding transcription. These models have been instrumental in improving the accuracy of automatic speech recognition systems.

Seq2Seq models are also widely used in chatbots and natural language understanding systems. They can generate natural language responses based on user input, providing human-like interactions. This technology has found applications in customer support, virtual assistants, and more. In the field of image captioning, Seq2Seq models combine visual and textual information to generate descriptive captions for images. The encoder processes the image, and the decoder generates a sentence describing the content. This has applications in image retrieval, content recommendation, and accessibility.

Seq2Seq models can be further enhanced with attention mechanisms, which enable the model to selectively focus on different parts of the input sequence while generating the output sequence. Attention mechanisms have proven effective in improving the quality of generated sequences and have become a standard component in many Seq2Seq architectures.

One common type of attention mechanism is the "soft" attention mechanism, which assigns a weight to each element in the input sequence based on its relevance to the current step of the decoder. The context vector used by the decoder is then a weighted sum of the encoder's hidden states, where the weights are determined by the attention mechanism. This allows the model to attend to different parts of the input sequence at each decoding step.

Another application of Seq2Seq models is in code generation and program synthesis. These models can take a high-level description or intent as input and generate executable code in various programming languages. This has implications for automating software development and simplifying programming tasks.

In the field of finance, Seq2Seq models can be used for time series forecasting and prediction of financial markets. These models can analyze historical financial data and generate predictions for stock prices, asset values, and economic indicators.

Seq2Seq models have also found applications in the healthcare industry, where they can assist in tasks such as medical report generation, disease diagnosis, and drug discovery. These models can process patient data, medical records, and clinical notes to provide valuable insights and recommendations.

Despite their effectiveness, Seq2Seq models have certain limitations. They require large amounts of training data and can be computationally intensive to train. Additionally, handling long sequences can be challenging, as it may lead to vanishing or exploding gradients during training.

In summary, Sequence-to-Sequence (Seq2Seq) models represent a versatile class of neural networks that excel in handling sequential data with varying input-output relationships. Their encoder-decoder architecture makes them suitable for tasks such as machine translation, text summarization, and speech recognition. With the incorporation of attention mechanisms, Seq2Seq models have achieved state-of-the-art results in various natural language processing and sequence generation applications. Their potential extends to fields like code generation, image captioning, finance, healthcare, and more, making them a valuable tool in the AI and machine learning toolkit.

Chapter 8: Transfer Learning and Pretrained Models

Leveraging pretrained models is a powerful technique in the field of deep learning and artificial intelligence. Next, we will explore the concept of pretrained models, how they work, and their applications across various domains, including computer vision, natural language processing, and more.

Pretrained models are neural network models that have been trained on a large dataset for a specific task before being fine-tuned for a new, related task. The idea behind pretrained models is to transfer knowledge learned from one task to another, often referred to as transfer learning. This approach can save significant time and computational resources compared to training a deep network from scratch.

The success of pretrained models is rooted in the ability of deep neural networks to learn rich, hierarchical representations of data. In the initial layers of a deep network, features learned are often general and can be applied to a wide range of tasks. These features capture fundamental patterns like edges, textures, and simple shapes.

In the context of computer vision, pretrained models are often based on convolutional neural networks (CNNs). These models are initially trained on massive image datasets, such as ImageNet, to learn a general understanding of visual features. The learned features in the early layers of these models are then fine-tuned for specific computer vision tasks, such as image classification, object detection, or image segmentation.

One of the most well-known pretrained models in computer vision is the ImageNet pretrained model, often based on architectures like VGG, ResNet, or Inception. These models achieve state-of-the-art results on image classification benchmarks and serve as strong starting points for various computer vision tasks.

In natural language processing (NLP), pretrained models have also revolutionized the field. NLP pretrained models are typically based on recurrent neural networks (RNNs), convolutional neural networks (CNNs), or more recently, transformer-based architectures. These models are pretrained on massive text corpora to learn contextual representations of language.

Transformers, in particular, have gained immense popularity in NLP. Models like BERT (Bidirectional Encoder Representations from Transformers) and GPT (Generative Pretrained Transformer) have set new benchmarks in various NLP tasks. BERT, for example, is pretrained on a massive amount of text data in a bidirectional manner, allowing it to understand the context of words in a sentence.

The idea of pretrained models extends beyond computer vision and NLP. In speech recognition, models like wav2vec and Listen, Attend, and Spell (LAS) have demonstrated significant improvements in automatic speech recognition tasks. These models leverage pretrained knowledge from large audio datasets, making them valuable for speech-related applications.

In the field of recommendation systems, pretrained models have also been applied. Collaborative filtering models pretrained on user-item interaction data can be fine-tuned for personalized recommendations. This approach can enhance the quality of recommendations for users with limited interaction history.

Leveraging pretrained models offers several advantages. Firstly, it reduces the need for extensive labeled data for training. This is especially valuable in scenarios where collecting labeled data is expensive or time-consuming. By starting with a pretrained model, practitioners can build upon existing knowledge and adapt it to their specific tasks.

Secondly, pretrained models often provide a strong initialization point for training. The features learned by the pretrained model in the early layers can capture general patterns and semantics of the data, making it easier for subsequent layers to specialize in the task-specific details.

Thirdly, pretrained models are often accompanied by prebuilt tools and libraries that simplify the process of fine-tuning and adapting the model to new tasks. These tools can include data preprocessing pipelines, training scripts, and evaluation metrics.

The concept of transfer learning through pretrained models has gained prominence in the research community and industry. Open-source initiatives have made pretrained models readily available, allowing researchers and developers to access and build upon the latest advancements in deep learning.

In computer vision, pretrained models are available in popular deep learning frameworks like TensorFlow and PyTorch. These frameworks provide pretrained weights for architectures like ResNet, Inception, and MobileNet, making it easy to use them in custom applications.

In NLP, pretrained models like BERT and GPT are available in various libraries, enabling researchers to leverage their power for a wide range of text-related tasks. These libraries offer user-friendly APIs for text preprocessing, fine-tuning, and inference.

The applications of pretrained models are vast. In computer vision, they can be used for tasks such as image classification, object detection, image segmentation, and even image generation. Fine-tuning a pretrained model on a specific dataset can quickly lead to state-of-the-art performance.

In NLP, pretrained models are used for sentiment analysis, text classification, named entity recognition, and machine translation, among others. Their ability to understand contextual language semantics has made them invaluable in understanding and generating human-like text.

In speech recognition, pretrained models are applied to automatic speech recognition (ASR) tasks, where they can convert spoken language into text. This has applications in transcription services, voice assistants, and more.

Recommendation systems leverage pretrained models for collaborative filtering and content-based recommendations. These models can provide users with personalized recommendations for products, content, and services.

In healthcare, pretrained models have been used for medical image analysis, disease diagnosis, and drug discovery. The ability to transfer knowledge from large medical datasets can assist in automating tasks and improving patient care.

Financial institutions use pretrained models for tasks like fraud detection, risk assessment, and algorithmic trading. These models can process large volumes of financial data and identify anomalies or patterns that human analysts might miss.

Despite the advantages and wide-ranging applications of pretrained models, there are some considerations to keep in mind. Fine-tuning pretrained models requires a good understanding of the specific task and dataset. In some cases, fine-tuning may involve extensive hyperparameter tuning and architectural adjustments.

Additionally, pretrained models can be computationally expensive to train or fine-tune, especially on large-scale datasets. Practitioners should be mindful of the computational resources and time required for training.

In summary, leveraging pretrained models is a transformative approach in the field of deep learning and artificial intelligence. These models, pretrained on large and diverse datasets, can transfer valuable knowledge to a wide range of tasks across computer vision, natural language processing, speech recognition, recommendation systems, healthcare, and finance. By building upon the foundation of pretrained models, researchers and developers can accelerate the development of state-of-the-art solutions and advance the capabilities of AI systems.

Fine-tuning is a crucial technique in the realm of deep learning and neural networks. Next, we will explore the concept of fine-tuning, its importance, and the steps involved in adapting pretrained models for specific tasks across various domains.

Fine-tuning refers to the process of taking a pretrained neural network model and adapting it for a new, task-specific purpose. The idea is to leverage the knowledge and features learned by the pretrained model and adjust them to better suit the requirements of the new task. Fine-tuning can save significant time and resources compared to training a model from scratch.

The pretrained model used for fine-tuning is often referred to as the "base model." This base model has typically been pretrained on a large and diverse dataset for a related task. For example, in computer vision, a base model might be pretrained on ImageNet for image classification, while in natural language processing, a base model could be pretrained on a large text corpus for language understanding.

Fine-tuning begins by initializing the model's parameters with the pretrained weights. This initialization provides the model with a strong starting point, as the pretrained weights already capture general features and patterns related to the task.

Once the base model is initialized, the next step is to replace or modify the final layers of the model to align it with the specific task. These final layers are often referred to as the "head" of the model and are task-specific. For example, in a computer vision task like object detection, the head might consist of layers responsible for predicting bounding boxes and class labels.

The base model's architecture and parameters, up to the final layers, are considered "frozen" during fine-tuning. This means that the weights of these layers remain fixed and do not change during the fine-tuning process. Freezing the base model prevents it from forgetting the valuable knowledge it has learned from the pretrained weights.

The task-specific head of the model is where most of the changes occur during fine-tuning. These layers are initialized with random weights and are trained on the new task's dataset. The number of layers and their complexity can vary depending on the task and the available data.

Fine-tuning typically involves training the model on the new task's dataset using a smaller learning rate than what was used during the initial pretrained training. This smaller learning rate ensures that the model's weights are updated gradually to adapt to the new task while preserving the knowledge from the pretrained model.

During fine-tuning, it's essential to use an appropriate loss function that matches the task's objective. For example, in an image classification task, a categorical cross-entropy loss might be used, while in a regression task, mean squared error could be more suitable.

Fine-tuning is highly valuable across various domains and tasks. In computer vision, it is common to fine-tune pretrained models for tasks such as object detection, image segmentation, and image captioning. By leveraging pretrained models, practitioners can quickly achieve state-of-the-art results on these tasks with less data and computational resources.

In natural language processing, fine-tuning pretrained language models has become a standard practice. Models like BERT, GPT, and RoBERTa have set new benchmarks in tasks like sentiment analysis, text classification, and named entity recognition. Fine-tuning allows these models to understand and generate human-like text in a wide range of applications.

In speech recognition, pretrained models are adapted for specific languages and dialects by fine-tuning on localized speech data. This ensures that the models can accurately transcribe spoken language, even in diverse linguistic environments.

Fine-tuning is also prevalent in recommendation systems, where models are customized to provide personalized recommendations. These models can be fine-tuned to consider user preferences, historical behavior, and context-specific factors, leading to more relevant recommendations.

In healthcare, fine-tuning pretrained models has applications in medical image analysis, disease diagnosis, and drug discovery. By fine-tuning on medical data, models can learn to identify specific pathologies and assist in clinical decision-making.

In autonomous vehicles, pretrained models are fine-tuned for tasks like object detection, lane detection, and pedestrian tracking. This adaptation allows self-driving cars to perceive their surroundings and make real-time decisions based on visual data.

Fine-tuning also plays a role in anomaly detection, where models are trained to identify deviations from normal behavior. These models can adapt to changing conditions and detect unusual patterns or events in various domains, including cybersecurity and manufacturing.

Despite its advantages, fine-tuning comes with considerations and challenges. Selecting the appropriate pretrained model is crucial, as it should have relevant knowledge for the target task. Choosing the right layers to freeze and modify requires a good understanding of the model's architecture and the task's requirements.

Fine-tuning on a small or unrepresentative dataset can lead to overfitting, as the model may not generalize well to new data. It is essential to have a sufficiently large and diverse dataset for fine-tuning, or consider techniques like data augmentation and transfer learning with multiple pretrained models.

Hyperparameter tuning is another aspect of fine-tuning that requires attention. Parameters like learning rate, batch size, and the number of epochs should be optimized to ensure effective fine-tuning.

Evaluating the fine-tuned model's performance is critical. Cross-validation and validation sets help assess the model's generalization ability and identify potential issues like overfitting.

In summary, fine-tuning is a crucial technique in deep learning that enables the adaptation of pretrained models for specific tasks across various domains. By leveraging the knowledge and features learned by pretrained models, practitioners can save time and resources while achieving state-of-the-art results. However, fine-tuning requires careful consideration of model selection, architecture, data, and hyperparameters to ensure success in the target task.

Chapter 9: Overcoming Common Deep Learning Challenges

Dealing with overfitting is a critical challenge in the field of machine learning and deep learning. Next, we will explore the concept of overfitting, its causes, and various techniques and strategies to mitigate its impact on model performance.

Overfitting occurs when a machine learning model learns to perform exceptionally well on the training data but fails to generalize effectively to new, unseen data. In essence, the model "memorizes" the training data instead of learning the underlying patterns and relationships within it.

The primary cause of overfitting is model complexity. When a model is excessively complex, it has the capacity to capture noise or random variations in the training data, which are not representative of the true underlying patterns. As a result, the model becomes overly specialized to the training data, leading to poor generalization.

A common symptom of overfitting is a significant gap between the model's performance on the training data and its performance on a validation or test dataset. While the model may achieve excellent accuracy on the training data, its accuracy drops considerably when evaluated on new, unseen data.

One fundamental technique to combat overfitting is to use a simpler model architecture. Simpler models have fewer parameters and are less likely to fit the noise in the training data. By reducing model complexity, the model is forced to focus on capturing the essential patterns and relationships in the data.

Another approach to address overfitting is to increase the amount of training data. Larger datasets provide more diverse examples and make it harder for the model to memorize the training data. This augmentation of data helps the model generalize better to unseen examples.

Regularization is a powerful tool for combating overfitting. Regularization techniques add penalty terms to the model's loss function, discouraging the model from assigning excessive importance to individual features or parameters. Common forms of regularization include L1 and L2 regularization, dropout, and early stopping.

L1 and L2 regularization add penalty terms to the loss function that encourage the model's weights to be smaller. This discourages the model from assigning high weights to individual features or parameters, reducing the risk of overfitting.

Dropout is a regularization technique that randomly drops a fraction of the neurons or connections during each training iteration. This helps prevent the model from relying too heavily on specific neurons or features, promoting a more balanced representation.

Early stopping involves monitoring the model's performance on a validation dataset during training. If the model's performance on the validation dataset starts to degrade after an initial improvement, training is halted to prevent overfitting.

Cross-validation is a valuable technique for assessing a model's generalization performance. Instead of relying on a single validation set, cross-validation involves dividing the data into multiple subsets and training and evaluating the model on different combinations of these subsets. This provides a more robust estimate of the model's performance and helps detect overfitting.

Ensemble methods are another approach to address overfitting. Ensemble methods combine the predictions of multiple models to make a final prediction. By combining diverse models, ensemble methods can reduce overfitting and improve generalization.

Bagging, boosting, and stacking are common ensemble techniques. Bagging involves training multiple models on random subsets of the data and averaging their predictions. Boosting focuses on training models sequentially, with each subsequent model trying to correct the errors of the previous ones. Stacking combines the predictions of multiple models as input to a final model.

Feature engineering is a critical aspect of preventing overfitting. Carefully selecting and transforming features can reduce the dimensionality of the input space and help the model focus on the most relevant information. Feature selection techniques, such as mutual information and recursive feature elimination, can help identify the most important features.

In deep learning, techniques like batch normalization and weight initialization can aid in reducing overfitting. Batch normalization helps stabilize the training process by normalizing the inputs to each layer. Weight initialization methods, like He initialization, can set appropriate initial values for the model's weights, improving convergence and reducing overfitting.

Data augmentation is a technique that artificially increases the size of the training dataset by applying various transformations to the original data. These transformations can include random rotations, translations, flips, and color adjustments. Data augmentation introduces variability into the training data, making it harder for the model to overfit.

Regularization techniques specific to deep learning include dropout and weight decay. Dropout randomly drops a fraction of the neurons during training, forcing the model to rely on a diverse set of neurons and reducing overfitting. Weight decay adds a penalty term to the loss function, encouraging smaller weights and preventing the model from fitting the training data too closely.

Hyperparameter tuning is an essential step in mitigating overfitting. Choosing appropriate hyperparameters, such as learning rate, batch size, and the number of layers, can significantly impact a model's generalization performance. Grid search and random search are common methods for hyperparameter optimization.

In summary, overfitting is a common challenge in machine learning and deep learning, and it occurs when a model performs well on training data but poorly on new, unseen data. Understanding the causes of overfitting and applying appropriate techniques, such as simplifying the model, using regularization, increasing data, and feature engineering, can help address this issue. Ensemble methods, feature selection, and hyperparameter tuning are additional tools that can improve a model's generalization performance. In deep learning, specific techniques like dropout, weight initialization, and batch normalization play a vital role in preventing overfitting and achieving better generalization.

Handling imbalanced data is a crucial consideration in the field of machine learning and data science. Next, we will explore the concept of imbalanced data, its challenges, and various techniques and strategies to address this issue and improve model performance.

Imbalanced data occurs when one class or category in a classification problem is significantly more prevalent than others. This imbalance can lead to biased model predictions, as the model may favor the majority class while neglecting the minority class.

One common scenario where imbalanced data arises is in medical diagnosis, where the occurrence of a rare disease is much lower than that of non-disease cases. Another example is fraud detection in financial transactions, where fraudulent transactions represent a small fraction of overall transactions.

The primary challenge of imbalanced data is that machine learning models tend to be biased towards the majority class. This is because models are designed to optimize overall accuracy, and classifying most instances as the majority class can achieve high accuracy even if the minority class is misclassified.

One of the first steps in handling imbalanced data is to carefully consider the evaluation metric. Accuracy is not an appropriate metric for imbalanced datasets, as it can be misleading. Instead, metrics like precision, recall, F1-score, and area under the receiver operating characteristic curve (AUC-ROC) are more informative for imbalanced classification problems.

Precision measures the ability of a model to correctly classify positive instances among all instances it predicts as positive. Recall, on the other hand, measures the ability to correctly classify positive instances among all actual positive instances.

The F1-score is the harmonic mean of precision and recall and provides a balanced measure of a model's performance. AUC-ROC quantifies the model's ability to distinguish between positive and negative instances, regardless of the class distribution.

Resampling is a common technique to address class imbalance. It involves either oversampling the minority class or undersampling the majority class to create a more balanced dataset.

Oversampling generates synthetic examples for the minority class by duplicating existing instances or generating new ones through techniques like bootstrapping or synthetic minority oversampling technique (SMOTE).

Undersampling, on the other hand, reduces the number of majority class instances by randomly removing samples. Care should be taken when undersampling to ensure that the reduced dataset remains representative of the overall distribution.

An alternative approach to resampling is the use of cost-sensitive learning. Cost-sensitive learning assigns different misclassification costs to different classes. It penalizes misclassifying the minority class more than the majority class, encouraging the model to prioritize the minority class.

Ensemble methods are another effective way to handle imbalanced data. Ensemble methods combine multiple models to make a final prediction. In the context of imbalanced data, ensembles can include techniques like bagging and boosting.

Bagging involves training multiple models on different subsets of the data and combining their predictions. This can reduce the impact of imbalanced classes and improve model generalization.

Boosting, on the other hand, focuses on training models sequentially, with each model giving more weight to instances that were misclassified by the previous ones. Boosting can be particularly effective for imbalanced datasets, as it emphasizes the minority class.

Modifying the decision threshold is a straightforward technique for handling imbalanced data. By adjusting the threshold for classifying instances as positive or negative, the model's precision and recall can be balanced.

Choosing a higher threshold increases precision but reduces recall, while selecting a lower threshold increases recall but reduces precision. The choice of threshold depends on the specific problem and the importance of precision and recall.

Anomaly detection methods can be applied when the minority class represents outliers or anomalies. These methods aim to identify instances that deviate significantly from the majority class. Techniques like one-class SVM, isolation forests, and autoencoders can be useful for anomaly detection.

Using different algorithms or models can also help address class imbalance. Certain algorithms, such as support vector machines (SVMs) and decision trees, can be sensitive to class distribution. Switching to algorithms that are less affected by class imbalance, like random forests or gradient boosting, can yield better results.

Feature engineering plays a crucial role in handling imbalanced data. By creating informative features, the model can better differentiate between classes. Feature selection techniques can help identify the most relevant features for classification.

Cost-sensitive learning involves assigning different misclassification costs to different classes. This approach encourages the model to prioritize the minority class by penalizing misclassifications more heavily.

Evaluation and validation are essential aspects of handling imbalanced data. Cross-validation and stratified sampling ensure that the model is evaluated properly and that the imbalance is preserved during training and testing.

In deep learning, techniques like weighted loss functions can be applied to give more importance to the minority class. By assigning higher weights to the minority class, the model is encouraged to focus on correctly classifying these instances.

Handling imbalanced data is a complex and problem-specific task. The choice of technique or combination of techniques depends on the nature of the data and the importance of different metrics. It is essential to experiment with various approaches and carefully evaluate the model's performance to find the most effective solution.

In summary, handling imbalanced data is a critical challenge in machine learning and data science. Imbalanced datasets can lead to biased model predictions and the misclassification of minority classes. Techniques such as resampling, cost-sensitive learning, ensemble methods, modifying decision thresholds, and feature engineering can help address this issue and improve model performance. Choosing the appropriate approach or combination of approaches depends on the specific problem and the desired balance between precision and recall.

Chapter 10: Real-World Applications and Future Trends in Deep Learning

Deep learning has emerged as a powerful tool in the field of healthcare, with the potential to transform diagnosis, treatment, and patient care. Next, we will explore the application of deep learning techniques in healthcare, highlighting the significant impact they have had and the challenges they face.

One of the primary areas where deep learning has made significant contributions is in medical image analysis. Convolutional neural networks (CNNs) have shown remarkable performance in tasks like detecting diseases from medical images. In radiology, CNNs are used to detect and classify abnormalities in X-rays, CT scans, and MRIs, aiding radiologists in their diagnoses.

In pathology, deep learning models have been developed to analyze histopathology slides, helping pathologists detect and classify diseases like cancer. These models can identify subtle patterns and anomalies that may be challenging to discern with the naked eye.

In cardiology, deep learning has been applied to electrocardiogram (ECG) analysis. Models can detect arrhythmias, predict cardiovascular events, and assist in diagnosing heart diseases.

Deep learning has also shown promise in medical imaging for ophthalmology. Retinal scans can be analyzed to detect conditions like diabetic retinopathy, glaucoma, and macular degeneration.

Natural language processing (NLP) techniques have been applied to electronic health records (EHRs) and clinical notes. Deep learning models can extract valuable information from unstructured text, aiding in clinical decision support, patient management, and research.

Drug discovery and development have also benefited from deep learning. Generative models can design novel molecules with desired properties, potentially accelerating drug discovery processes.

In genomics, deep learning models can predict genetic risk factors for diseases, analyze DNA sequences, and identify potential drug targets.

Remote patient monitoring has become more effective with the use of wearable devices and sensors. Deep learning can analyze data from these devices to detect anomalies, monitor chronic conditions, and provide timely interventions.

Despite the many successes, deep learning in healthcare comes with several challenges. One major concern is the need for large and high-quality datasets. Training deep learning models typically requires vast amounts of labeled data, which may be scarce or expensive to obtain in the medical field.

Interpreting deep learning models is another challenge. Understanding how a model arrives at a particular diagnosis or prediction is critical for gaining the trust of healthcare professionals. Methods for explaining and visualizing model decisions are an active area of research.

Ensuring the privacy and security of patient data is paramount in healthcare. Deep learning models must be developed with robust privacy safeguards to protect sensitive information.

Regulatory and ethical considerations also play a significant role. Deep learning models must meet stringent regulatory requirements, and ethical concerns related to bias, fairness, and transparency need to be addressed.

Integration into healthcare systems is another challenge. Adopting deep learning models into clinical workflows and ensuring their compatibility with existing systems can be complex.

Continual model updating and validation are necessary to ensure that deep learning models perform reliably in real-world clinical settings.

Despite these challenges, the potential benefits of deep learning in healthcare are immense. The ability to provide early and accurate diagnoses, predict disease progression, and recommend personalized treatments can significantly improve patient outcomes.

Furthermore, deep learning can help reduce healthcare costs by automating routine tasks, improving efficiency, and reducing errors.

In summary, deep learning has the potential to revolutionize healthcare by enhancing medical image analysis, enabling better disease detection and diagnosis, improving treatment plans, and optimizing patient care. Despite the challenges, ongoing research and collaboration between the healthcare and machine learning communities continue to advance the field and unlock new opportunities for improving human health and well-being.

Exploring the ever-evolving landscape of deep learning research reveals a plethora of emerging trends and innovations that are shaping the future of artificial intelligence. One of the most prominent trends is the development of increasingly large and complex neural network architectures.

These architectures, often referred to as "mega-models," have billions or even trillions of parameters and require immense computational resources for training. The pursuit of larger models is driven by the desire to achieve state-of-the-art results on a wide range of tasks, from natural language understanding to image recognition.

One example of a mega-model is OpenAI's GPT-3, which demonstrated remarkable natural language processing capabilities. GPT-3 can generate coherent and contextually relevant text, making it a valuable tool for tasks like language translation, content generation, and chatbot development.
The rise of mega-models has led to new challenges in terms of scalability, efficiency, and ethical considerations. Researchers are exploring techniques to make training and deployment of such models more sustainable and accessible. Efforts are also being made to improve the energy efficiency of deep learning, as training large models consumes significant computational power. Research into quantization, model compression, and hardware acceleration is ongoing to address these concerns.

Another emerging trend in deep learning research is the exploration of self-supervised learning. Self-supervised learning is a paradigm where models learn from unlabeled data by generating their own labels or objectives.
This approach has shown promising results in natural language processing and computer vision tasks. Self-supervised models can pretrain on large datasets and fine-tune on specific tasks, reducing the need for extensive labeled data.
Transformers, a type of neural architecture, have gained widespread popularity in various deep learning applications. Originally designed for natural language processing,

transformers have been adapted and extended to other domains.

For example, vision transformers (ViTs) apply transformer architectures to image data, achieving competitive performance in image classification and object detection tasks. This cross-domain application of transformers highlights their versatility and potential for future research.

Another noteworthy trend is the integration of deep learning with reinforcement learning in what is known as deep reinforcement learning (DRL). DRL combines neural networks with reinforcement learning algorithms to enable agents to learn complex behaviors through interaction with their environments.

This approach has yielded impressive results in areas like autonomous robotics, game playing, and healthcare. DRL agents have achieved superhuman performance in games like Go, Dota 2, and StarCraft II, showcasing the potential of combining deep learning and reinforcement learning.

Ethics, fairness, and bias in deep learning have become prominent concerns in recent years. Researchers are increasingly focused on addressing biases present in both training data and model outputs.

Efforts are underway to develop tools and frameworks for auditing and mitigating bias in machine learning models. Ensuring fairness and ethical use of AI technologies is an ongoing challenge that requires interdisciplinary collaboration and regulatory guidelines.

Explainability and interpretability of deep learning models are also areas of active research. Understanding why a model makes a particular decision is crucial for gaining user trust and for making informed decisions in high-stakes applications.

Research into techniques for explaining model predictions, such as attention mechanisms and saliency maps, aims to make deep learning models more transparent and interpretable.

The deployment of deep learning in real-world applications has led to increased attention on robustness and adversarial attacks. Deep learning models are vulnerable to adversarial examples—inputs that are intentionally crafted to mislead the model's predictions.

Research in adversarial machine learning seeks to enhance the robustness of models and develop defenses against adversarial attacks. This is particularly important in safety-critical domains like autonomous driving and healthcare.

The synergy between neuroscience and deep learning research is another emerging trend. Researchers are drawing inspiration from the brain's structure and functioning to improve the design and capabilities of artificial neural networks.

Neuromorphic computing, which emulates the brain's architecture, holds promise for energy-efficient and brain-inspired computing systems.

The exploration of novel applications for deep learning is ongoing. From drug discovery to climate modeling, deep learning is being applied to address complex and pressing global challenges.

Deep learning's potential to accelerate scientific discovery and innovation is being recognized across disciplines.

Collaboration between academia, industry, and government agencies is crucial for advancing deep learning research. Open-source platforms, shared datasets, and collaboration initiatives are fostering a vibrant research community.

In summary, the field of deep learning is continually evolving, driven by emerging trends and innovations. Mega-models, self-supervised learning, transformers, deep reinforcement learning, ethics and fairness, explainability, adversarial machine learning, neuroscience-inspired research, and novel applications are all shaping the future of deep learning.

As researchers continue to push the boundaries of what is possible, deep learning will likely play an increasingly central role in addressing complex problems and driving technological advancements across a wide range of domains.

BOOK 2
MASTERING COMPUTER VISION WITH DEEP LEARNING

ROB BOTWRIGHT

Chapter 1: Introduction to Computer Vision and Deep Learning

The intersection of computer vision and deep learning has revolutionized the field of artificial intelligence by enabling machines to interpret and understand visual information. Computer vision, as a discipline, focuses on teaching machines to extract meaningful insights from images and videos, mimicking the human ability to perceive and interpret visual data.

Deep learning, on the other hand, is a subset of machine learning that uses neural networks with multiple layers to automatically learn and represent data features. The combination of deep learning and computer vision has led to significant advancements in various applications, ranging from object recognition to medical image analysis.

One of the fundamental challenges in computer vision is image classification, where the goal is to assign a label or category to an input image. Deep learning models, particularly convolutional neural networks (CNNs), have achieved remarkable accuracy in image classification tasks.

CNNs can automatically learn hierarchical features from raw pixel data, enabling them to recognize patterns, shapes, and textures in images. This capability has been crucial in fields like autonomous driving, where CNNs are used to identify pedestrians, vehicles, and road signs from camera feeds.

Object detection is another vital task in computer vision, where the objective is to identify and locate objects within an image. Deep learning models, including region-based and single-shot detectors, have significantly improved object detection accuracy.

These models can identify multiple objects in complex scenes and provide bounding box coordinates, making them valuable for applications like surveillance, robotics, and content-based image retrieval.

Semantic segmentation takes object detection a step further by assigning a pixel-level label to each object in an image. Deep learning models, especially fully convolutional networks (FCNs) and U-Net architectures, excel in semantic segmentation tasks.

These models can create pixel-wise masks that precisely outline object boundaries, making them useful in medical image analysis, where accurate organ and tumor segmentation is crucial.

The ability to understand the spatial relationships between objects in an image is essential in tasks like image captioning and scene understanding. Deep learning models, such as recurrent neural networks (RNNs) and transformers, have been applied to these challenges.

By combining CNNs for feature extraction and RNNs for sequential data modeling, models can generate descriptive captions for images, making them accessible for visually impaired individuals and enhancing content indexing.

Computer vision also plays a vital role in biometrics and security. Facial recognition, fingerprint analysis, and iris scanning are examples of biometric authentication methods that leverage deep learning for accurate identification.

Deep learning models can extract unique features from biometric data, making them suitable for applications like access control, border security, and mobile device authentication.

The healthcare industry has benefited significantly from the intersection of computer vision and deep learning. Medical image analysis tasks, such as diagnosing diseases from X-rays, MRIs, and CT scans, have seen improved accuracy and efficiency with deep learning models.

These models can detect anomalies, quantify disease progression, and assist healthcare professionals in making more informed decisions.

Furthermore, the use of deep learning in telemedicine and remote patient monitoring has become increasingly important, especially in the context of global health crises.

The application of computer vision and deep learning in autonomous robotics is a rapidly growing field. Self-driving cars rely heavily on computer vision systems, using deep learning models to perceive the environment, detect obstacles, and make driving decisions in real time.

Robots equipped with cameras and sensors can use computer vision and deep learning to navigate and interact with their surroundings, making them versatile tools in industrial automation, logistics, and healthcare.

Augmented reality (AR) and virtual reality (VR) experiences also benefit from computer vision and deep learning. AR applications overlay digital information on the physical world, requiring accurate spatial tracking and object recognition.

Deep learning models can enhance AR capabilities by recognizing objects, people, and landmarks, allowing for more immersive and interactive experiences.

In the world of e-commerce and retail, computer vision and deep learning are transforming the shopping experience. Visual search engines enable users to search for products using images rather than text, making online shopping more intuitive and convenient.

Retailers can use computer vision to analyze customer behavior in stores, optimize shelf placement, and personalize marketing efforts.

The fusion of computer vision and deep learning has also led to breakthroughs in creative industries. Artists and designers use generative adversarial networks (GANs) to create realistic images, videos, and 3D models.

These models can generate new artwork, simulate realistic environments, and even help in the design of products and fashion.

Despite the remarkable progress, the field of computer vision and deep learning faces ongoing challenges. Robustness and reliability are critical concerns, as deep learning models can be sensitive to variations in lighting, pose, and environmental conditions.

Ensuring the privacy and security of visual data is another challenge, particularly in applications like surveillance and facial recognition.

Interpreting deep learning models is an area of active research, as understanding their decision-making processes is essential for transparency and accountability.

Ethical considerations related to bias and fairness in computer vision algorithms require continuous attention to avoid reinforcing existing societal biases.

Continual advancements in hardware and software technologies, as well as interdisciplinary collaboration, are driving the field forward.

In summary, the intersection of computer vision and deep learning has revolutionized how machines perceive and understand visual information. From image classification and object detection to semantic segmentation and biometrics, deep learning has enabled remarkable achievements across various domains.

While challenges remain, the ongoing research and innovation in this field promise to further enhance our ability to harness the power of visual data for the benefit of society.

Applications of computer vision in the modern world span a wide range of industries and domains, transforming the way we interact with technology and the physical environment. In healthcare, computer vision plays a pivotal role in medical imaging, aiding in the early detection and diagnosis of various diseases.

Radiology benefits from computer-aided diagnosis (CAD) systems that assist radiologists in interpreting X-rays, CT scans, and MRIs, improving accuracy and efficiency.

Pathology leverages computer vision for the analysis of histopathology slides, enabling the identification and classification of cancerous tissues with precision.

In ophthalmology, retinal scans are analyzed to detect and monitor conditions like diabetic retinopathy and macular degeneration, helping prevent vision loss.

Surveillance and security are areas where computer vision has a profound impact, enhancing public safety and crime prevention. CCTV cameras equipped with computer vision algorithms can identify suspicious activities, track individuals, and alert authorities to potential threats.

Facial recognition technology is employed for access control, border security, and identity verification, making it a powerful tool in law enforcement and airport security.

Traffic management and smart transportation systems rely on computer vision for traffic monitoring, congestion detection, and automated toll collection.

Autonomous vehicles use computer vision to perceive their surroundings, identify road signs, pedestrians, and obstacles, enabling safe and efficient self-driving capabilities.

In agriculture, computer vision helps optimize crop management, improve yields, and reduce resource wastage. Drones equipped with cameras and computer vision algorithms monitor crop health, detect pests, and assess soil conditions.

Computer vision in retail is transforming the shopping experience, both in physical stores and online. Visual search engines allow customers to find products by uploading images, making online shopping more convenient.

In-store analytics use computer vision to track customer movements, optimize shelf layouts, and personalize marketing efforts based on shopper behavior.

The fashion industry benefits from virtual try-on experiences, where customers can visualize how clothing and accessories will look on them before making a purchase.

Quality control and manufacturing processes are significantly improved with the integration of computer vision. Automated visual inspection systems can detect defects in products, ensuring high-quality standards and reducing production costs.

Computer vision in robotics enhances the capabilities of robots in various applications. Robotic vision systems enable robots to navigate complex environments, manipulate objects, and interact with humans safely.

In the entertainment and creative industries, computer vision contributes to visual effects, animation, and augmented reality experiences. Face tracking and motion capture technologies enable realistic character animation in movies and video games.

Augmented reality (AR) apps overlay digital information on the real world, enhancing entertainment, education, and training.

Environmental monitoring and conservation efforts benefit from computer vision. Drones equipped with cameras and image recognition software can monitor wildlife populations, detect illegal poaching activities, and track changes in ecosystems.

In the construction and architecture sectors, computer vision aids in project management and design. Drones and cameras can create 3D models of construction sites, monitor progress, and identify safety hazards. Computer vision is also making a significant impact on accessibility and inclusivity. Text-to-speech systems use optical character recognition (OCR) to convert printed text into speech for individuals with visual impairments.

Gesture recognition technology allows users to control computers and devices through hand and body movements, providing alternative interfaces for those with mobility challenges. Art restoration and preservation benefit from computer vision techniques. High-resolution imaging and analysis help conservators restore and protect valuable artworks, uncovering hidden details and detecting deterioration.

In sports, computer vision enhances athlete performance analysis and officiating. Cameras and computer vision algorithms track player movements, analyze tactics, and provide instant replays during live broadcasts.

Human-computer interaction is transformed by computer vision in the form of gesture recognition, facial expression analysis, and eye-tracking technology.

In archaeology and cultural heritage preservation, computer vision assists in the documentation and analysis of ancient artifacts and archaeological sites.

Computer vision in finance includes applications like fraud detection and automated document processing. Machine learning models analyze financial transactions to detect fraudulent activities, while optical character recognition (OCR) extracts information from documents for automated data entry.

These examples illustrate the wide-reaching impact of computer vision in today's modern world, enhancing productivity, safety, accessibility, and creativity across diverse fields and industries.

The continuous advancement of computer vision techniques, combined with the increasing availability of high-quality image and video data, promises to unlock even more innovative applications in the future, shaping how we interact with technology and the world around us.

Chapter 2: Foundations of Image Processing and Feature Extraction

In the world of computer vision and image processing, understanding how images are represented and manipulated is fundamental. Images, at their core, are composed of pixels, which are the smallest units of an image, each containing information about color and intensity.

These pixels are arranged in a grid-like structure, forming the basis of the image. The resolution of an image determines the number of pixels it contains, with higher resolutions providing finer detail.

Color images are typically represented using the RGB color model, where each pixel is a combination of Red, Green, and Blue channels. By varying the intensity of each channel, a wide spectrum of colors can be created.

Grayscale images, on the other hand, have only one channel, representing the intensity of light at each pixel. Grayscale images are often used when color information is unnecessary or when simplifying the processing pipeline.

Digital images can be stored in various file formats, such as JPEG, PNG, and GIF, each with its own compression and quality considerations. The choice of format depends on factors like image content and intended use.

Image processing encompasses a wide range of techniques for manipulating and enhancing images. One fundamental operation is spatial filtering, which involves applying a filter or kernel to an image to modify its pixel values.

Filters can be used for tasks like blurring, sharpening, edge detection, and noise reduction. Convolution is the mathematical operation at the heart of spatial filtering.

Another common image processing operation is resizing, where an image is scaled up or down to a different resolution. Interpolation methods are used to estimate pixel values at the new size.

Histogram equalization is a technique for enhancing the contrast of an image by redistributing pixel intensities. It is particularly useful for improving the visibility of details in images with poor contrast.

Morphological operations involve the manipulation of image shapes and structures. Erosion and dilation are two basic morphological operations used for tasks like noise removal and object segmentation.

Image segmentation is the process of partitioning an image into distinct regions or objects based on certain criteria. Segmentation is often a critical step in computer vision tasks like object recognition.

Thresholding is a simple yet effective segmentation technique that separates objects from the background by setting a threshold on pixel intensity.

Clustering algorithms, such as k-means, can group pixels with similar characteristics into clusters, aiding in the separation of objects.

Edge detection algorithms identify the boundaries of objects within an image. Edges are areas of rapid intensity change and are essential for object recognition and shape analysis.

Feature extraction is the process of capturing relevant information from an image to represent its content. Features can be simple, like color histograms, or complex, like deep learning-based representations.

Geometric transformations, such as rotation, translation, and scaling, allow for image alignment and registration.

Image enhancement techniques, like gamma correction and contrast stretching, adjust pixel values to improve visual quality.

Image stitching combines multiple images into a single, larger panorama, often used in photography and virtual reality.

Noise reduction methods, such as median filtering and Gaussian smoothing, help remove unwanted artifacts from images.

Inpainting is a technique used to fill in missing or damaged regions of an image based on surrounding information.

Super-resolution aims to enhance image resolution beyond its original capabilities, often using deep learning-based models.

Image compression reduces the file size of an image while preserving visual quality, making it suitable for storage and transmission.

Color manipulation techniques, like color balance and color correction, adjust the color appearance of an image.

Texture analysis focuses on characterizing the repetitive patterns and structures in images, important for tasks like material recognition.

Image registration aligns two or more images to a common coordinate system, essential for medical imaging and remote sensing.

Image restoration aims to recover the true underlying image from a degraded or noisy version, using techniques like deconvolution.

Image understanding goes beyond basic image processing, involving higher-level tasks like object detection, recognition, and scene analysis.

Deep learning models, such as convolutional neural networks (CNNs), have achieved remarkable results in image understanding tasks.

Object detection algorithms, like YOLO and Faster R-CNN, locate and classify objects within an image, enabling applications like autonomous driving and surveillance.

Image recognition models classify objects or scenes within an image and are used in applications like image search and content tagging.

Scene understanding involves parsing an image to identify objects, their relationships, and the overall context.

Semantic segmentation assigns a label to each pixel in an image, enabling fine-grained scene understanding.

Generative models, like GANs and VAEs, can create new images based on learned patterns and styles, used in art generation and data augmentation.

Image captioning combines computer vision and natural language processing to generate textual descriptions of images.

Understanding and manipulating images is a fundamental aspect of computer vision and image processing. From basic operations like filtering and resizing to advanced tasks like object recognition and generative modeling, the field continues to evolve, enabling a wide range of applications across various domains. Feature extraction techniques in computer vision play a critical role in transforming raw image data into meaningful and actionable information. These techniques are essential for tasks like object detection, image recognition, and pattern analysis.

Features are distinctive and relevant characteristics extracted from an image that capture its essential information. One of the simplest feature extraction methods is edge detection, which identifies the boundaries or edges of objects within an image.

Edge detection algorithms, such as the Canny edge detector, Sobel operator, and Prewitt operator, highlight regions with significant intensity changes. Edges are crucial for recognizing object boundaries and shapes.

Another common feature extraction method is corner detection, which identifies key points or corners in an image.

Corners are locations where two or more edges intersect, making them important for image registration and tracking.

The Harris corner detector and Shi-Tomasi corner detector are popular techniques for corner detection. They evaluate the change in intensity around a pixel and select points with strong responses.

Texture features describe the spatial arrangement of pixel intensities and are used to characterize the texture of surfaces. Texture extraction methods include local binary patterns (LBP), gray-level co-occurrence matrices (GLCM), and Gabor filters.

Color features capture information about the distribution and properties of colors in an image. Color histograms, color moments, and color correlograms are examples of color feature extraction techniques.

Histogram-based features represent the frequency distribution of pixel values in an image channel. They provide insights into the dominant colors and their distribution.

Moment-based features capture statistics about the color distribution, including mean, variance, and skewness. Moments are used to describe the overall color characteristics of an image.

Correlogram-based features consider the spatial relationships between colors in an image. They provide information about how color values are correlated at different distances.

Texture features, color features, and edge features can be combined to create powerful feature vectors for image analysis. These feature vectors are used as input to machine learning algorithms for tasks like image classification and object recognition.

Scale-invariant feature transform (SIFT) is a feature extraction technique that identifies key points in an image and extracts distinctive descriptors. SIFT is robust to changes in scale, rotation, and illumination, making it valuable for object recognition.

Speeded-Up Robust Features (SURF) is a variant of SIFT that offers faster feature extraction while maintaining robustness.

Local feature descriptors like SIFT and SURF are used in applications like image matching, panoramic stitching, and augmented reality.

Histogram of Oriented Gradients (HOG) is a feature extraction technique used primarily for object detection in images. HOG describes the local shape and appearance of objects by analyzing the distribution of gradient orientations. HOG features are commonly employed in pedestrian detection systems, face recognition, and other object detection tasks.

Another popular feature extraction technique is the use of deep convolutional neural networks (CNNs). CNNs automatically learn hierarchical features from raw image data through a series of convolutional and pooling layers.

The features learned by CNNs are highly discriminative and are used in various computer vision tasks like image classification, object detection, and image segmentation.

Convolutional Neural Networks extract features at different levels of abstraction, starting from simple edges and textures and progressing to complex object parts and high-level concepts.

Transfer learning is a powerful approach in feature extraction, where pre-trained CNN models are fine-tuned on specific tasks or datasets. Transfer learning leverages the knowledge and features learned from large-scale datasets, such as ImageNet, to boost the performance of specialized tasks.

Principal Component Analysis (PCA) is a dimensionality reduction technique used for feature extraction. PCA transforms the original feature space into a lower-dimensional space while preserving the most significant variance.

PCA is employed to reduce the computational complexity of feature vectors and enhance the efficiency of machine learning models.

Local Binary Patterns (LBP) is a texture feature extraction method that characterizes the local patterns of pixel intensities. LBP is used in texture analysis, facial recognition, and texture classification.

Sparse coding is a feature extraction technique that represents an image as a linear combination of a small number of basis functions. Sparse coding learns a dictionary of basis functions that capture essential image structures.

Bag of Visual Words (BoVW) is a technique used in image classification and object recognition. BoVW represents an image as a histogram of visual words, which are learned from a set of local features.

Feature extraction is a crucial step in content-based image retrieval systems, where images are indexed and retrieved based on their visual content.

In summary, feature extraction techniques in computer vision are essential for transforming raw image data into meaningful representations. These representations capture distinctive characteristics of images and enable tasks like object detection, image recognition, and texture analysis.

From simple edge and corner detection to deep learning-based feature extraction, the field of computer vision continues to advance, offering a rich toolkit of methods for extracting valuable information from images.

Chapter 3: Building Convolutional Neural Networks (CNNs) for Image Classification

Understanding convolutional layers in Convolutional Neural Networks (CNNs) is crucial for grasping the core architectural elements that enable these networks to excel in tasks like image recognition, object detection, and image segmentation. Convolutional layers are one of the fundamental building blocks of CNNs, inspired by the human visual system's ability to recognize visual patterns.

At their essence, convolutional layers consist of a set of learnable filters or kernels that slide over the input data to extract features. These filters capture different characteristics of the input, such as edges, textures, or more complex patterns.

The operation performed by convolutional layers is known as convolution, which involves element-wise multiplication of the filter weights and a local region of the input, followed by summation. This process generates feature maps, which represent the presence of specific features within the input data.

Convolutional layers have several essential properties that make them well-suited for visual tasks. One key property is parameter sharing, where the same filter is applied to multiple locations in the input.

Parameter sharing significantly reduces the number of learnable weights in the network, making CNNs more efficient and effective for handling large and complex images.

Stride is another critical property of convolutional layers, which determines the step size at which the filters move over the input. Stride affects the size of the feature maps and, consequently, the spatial resolution of the network.

Pooling layers are often employed in CNNs following convolutional layers to reduce the spatial dimensions of the feature maps while preserving important features. Common pooling operations include max-pooling and average-pooling, which downsample the feature maps by selecting the maximum or average value within local regions.

Convolutional layers can be stacked to form deep networks, enabling the extraction of hierarchical features. The early layers capture low-level features like edges and textures, while deeper layers represent more abstract and complex patterns.

The depth of a CNN, determined by the number of convolutional layers, contributes to its ability to learn increasingly sophisticated representations.

In practice, CNNs are trained to learn filters that are highly tuned to specific features within the data. These filters are initialized with random values and updated during training using techniques like backpropagation and gradient descent.

The process of training a CNN involves feeding it labeled data and adjusting the filter weights to minimize the difference between the predicted outputs and the ground truth labels. This iterative optimization process enables the network to learn meaningful features for the task at hand.

Convolutional layers are not limited to single-channel images but can also handle multi-channel inputs, such as RGB color images. In this case, each filter is applied independently to each input channel, producing a separate set of feature maps for each channel.

The resulting feature maps are then combined, often using element-wise addition, to form a single feature map. Multi-channel inputs allow CNNs to capture rich and diverse information from color images.

Strided convolutions and pooling layers enable CNNs to reduce the spatial dimensions of feature maps while increasing their depth. This reduction in spatial resolution is essential for capturing higher-level features and reducing computational complexity.

The combination of convolutional layers, pooling layers, and fully connected layers allows CNNs to learn hierarchical representations of data. Convolutional layers capture local features, pooling layers aggregate information, and fully connected layers perform classification or regression tasks.

One of the remarkable properties of CNNs is their ability to automatically learn hierarchical features from raw data. This feature learning process is a crucial factor in their success in computer vision tasks.

Convolutional layers have demonstrated their effectiveness in various computer vision challenges. For instance, in image classification tasks, CNNs can learn to recognize objects and scenes from images with high accuracy.

In object detection tasks, CNNs can identify and locate multiple objects within an image, often with bounding box predictions.

In image segmentation, CNNs can assign a label to each pixel, segmenting the image into regions corresponding to different object categories.

CNNs have also been applied to problems like facial recognition, medical image analysis, autonomous driving, and more.

While convolutional layers have proven to be highly effective, CNNs are not without their challenges. One challenge is the need for large amounts of labeled training data to train deep networks effectively.

Training deep CNNs requires substantial computational resources, which can be a limitation for researchers and developers without access to powerful hardware.

Another challenge is the risk of overfitting, where the network performs well on the training data but poorly on new, unseen data. Regularization techniques, dropout, and data augmentation are used to mitigate overfitting.

Understanding convolutional layers is essential for designing and training effective CNNs. These layers enable the network to learn hierarchical representations of data, capture relevant features, and excel in various computer vision tasks. The ability to automatically learn and extract meaningful features from raw data makes CNNs a foundational technology in the field of computer vision and continues to drive advancements in image analysis and understanding.

In summary, convolutional layers in CNNs are a fundamental component of deep learning for computer vision. Their ability to learn and apply filters to input data, coupled with parameter sharing and strided operations, makes them a powerful tool for extracting features and patterns from images and other multi-channel data.

The hierarchical representation learning enabled by convolutional layers has transformed the field of computer vision and continues to be a driving force in its evolution.

Training a Convolutional Neural Network (CNN) for image classification is a complex but essential process in the field of computer vision. It involves teaching the network to recognize and differentiate between different objects or classes within images.

The first step in training a CNN is to gather a labeled dataset, which consists of images along with their corresponding class labels. This dataset serves as the foundation for the network to learn from and make predictions.

Data preprocessing is a crucial stage before training, where images are typically resized, normalized, and augmented.

Resizing ensures that all images are of the same dimensions, making them compatible with the CNN architecture.

Normalization helps standardize the pixel values, usually by scaling them to a range between 0 and 1 or -1 and 1, which aids in training stability.

Data augmentation involves applying random transformations to the images, such as rotations, flips, and translations. This helps increase the dataset's diversity and makes the model more robust to variations in the input.

The next step is to design the architecture of the CNN, which includes defining the number of layers, the size of the filters, and the architecture's depth. Common CNN architectures include LeNet, AlexNet, VGG, and more recent ones like ResNet and Inception.

The architecture choice depends on the complexity of the task and the available computational resources. For simpler tasks, a smaller network may suffice, while more complex tasks may require deeper and more complex architectures.

Once the architecture is defined, the next step is to initialize the network's weights. Random initialization is a common practice, but it's also possible to start with pre-trained weights on a related task, such as ImageNet.

Training a CNN involves optimizing its weights to minimize a loss function. The loss function quantifies the difference between the predicted class probabilities and the actual class labels in the training data.

The optimization process aims to adjust the network's weights to make its predictions closer to the ground truth labels. Stochastic Gradient Descent (SGD) and variants like Adam and RMSprop are popular optimization algorithms used for this purpose.

During training, the dataset is divided into mini-batches, and the network's weights are updated iteratively. Each mini-batch is forward-propagated through the network to compute predictions, and then backward-propagated to calculate gradients.

Gradients indicate the direction and magnitude of weight adjustments needed to reduce the loss. The learning rate determines the step size during weight updates, and it is a critical hyperparameter to tune.

Regularization techniques, such as dropout and weight decay, are often applied during training to prevent overfitting. Dropout randomly deactivates a fraction of neurons during each forward pass, while weight decay adds a penalty to large weight values.

Monitoring the training progress is essential, and this is typically done by evaluating the network's performance on a separate validation dataset. The validation dataset helps detect overfitting and allows for early stopping if the model's performance begins to degrade.

Training a CNN can take a considerable amount of time, especially for deep networks and large datasets. This process may involve hundreds or thousands of epochs, depending on the task's complexity and the convergence rate.

Once the training is complete, the final step is evaluating the CNN on a test dataset that it has never seen before. This provides an unbiased estimate of the model's generalization performance.

Common evaluation metrics for image classification tasks include accuracy, precision, recall, and F1-score. These metrics help assess the model's ability to correctly classify images and handle class imbalances.

Fine-tuning is another strategy that can be applied after training. This involves adjusting the model's weights using a smaller learning rate on a subset of the data or a different dataset.

Fine-tuning is useful when the model needs to adapt to specific characteristics of a new dataset or task without starting training from scratch.

Training a CNN is an iterative process that often requires hyperparameter tuning and experimentation. The choice of architecture, optimization algorithm, learning rate, and regularization techniques significantly impact the model's performance.

Transfer learning is a powerful approach that leverages pre-trained CNNs on large datasets to bootstrap the training process for new tasks. By using a pre-trained model as a feature extractor or fine-tuning some layers, transfer learning accelerates training and improves performance, particularly when data is limited.

Data quality is crucial for training a CNN successfully. Noisy or mislabeled data can lead to poor model performance, and data cleaning and validation are essential steps in the process. Training a CNN for image classification is a computationally intensive task. Training deep networks often requires specialized hardware, such as Graphics Processing Units (GPUs) or dedicated AI accelerators.

In summary, training a CNN for image classification involves several critical steps, from data collection and preprocessing to model architecture design, weight initialization, optimization, and evaluation. It's an iterative process that requires careful consideration of hyperparameters and techniques to achieve the desired performance on the task at hand.

With the increasing availability of large datasets and advances in deep learning frameworks, training CNNs has become more accessible, enabling a wide range of applications in image recognition, object detection, medical imaging, and more.

Chapter 4: Object Detection and Localization with CNNs

Object detection techniques are a fundamental component of computer vision, enabling machines to identify and locate objects within images and videos. This capability has numerous applications, from autonomous vehicles and surveillance systems to medical image analysis and content-based image retrieval.

One of the earliest and simplest object detection techniques is template matching, where a template or pattern is compared to different regions of an image to find instances of the template. While straightforward, template matching is limited in its ability to handle variations in scale, rotation, and lighting.

Histogram-based methods, such as the Histogram of Oriented Gradients (HOG), capture object shapes by analyzing the distribution of gradient orientations in an image. HOG is particularly effective in pedestrian detection and has been widely used in face detection as well.

Another popular approach is the use of Haar-like features combined with a cascaded classifier, as seen in Viola-Jones face detection. This technique employs a series of simple rectangular features and an efficient cascading classifier to rapidly identify objects.

More recently, machine learning-based methods have gained prominence in object detection. These methods leverage annotated training data to learn discriminative features and classification models.

Sliding window-based approaches, like the Deformable Part Model (DPM), divide an image into a grid of windows and classify each window as containing an object or not. These methods are effective but can be computationally intensive due to the large number of windows to evaluate.

The introduction of Convolutional Neural Networks (CNNs) revolutionized object detection. CNN-based detectors, such as Region-based CNNs (R-CNN) and its variants like Fast R-CNN and Faster R-CNN, excel in both accuracy and efficiency. R-CNNs use selective search to propose regions of interest in an image, which are then passed through a CNN to classify and refine object locations. Fast R-CNN improves speed by sharing computations across regions.

Faster R-CNN introduces Region Proposal Networks (RPNs) that predict objectness scores and bounding box coordinates directly, tightly integrating region proposal and classification.

Single Shot MultiBox Detector (SSD) and You Only Look Once (YOLO) are two popular object detection architectures. SSD performs detection at multiple scales, using different aspect ratio anchor boxes, while YOLO divides the image into a grid and predicts bounding boxes and class probabilities for each cell.

YOLO is known for its real-time performance, making it suitable for applications like real-time object tracking and autonomous driving.

Another influential approach is RetinaNet, which addresses the challenge of detecting objects at different scales with a single network. RetinaNet introduces the focal loss to address class imbalance issues common in object detection.

One-shot and few-shot object detection aim to detect objects with very limited training data. These techniques are valuable in scenarios where collecting extensive labeled data is challenging.

Meta-learning and Siamese networks are used to learn feature embeddings that can generalize to unseen object categories with minimal examples.

Object detection techniques are not limited to 2D images but also extend to 3D object detection in point clouds or voxel grids. These methods are crucial for applications like autonomous vehicles and robotics.

Light Detection and Ranging (LiDAR) sensors and depth cameras are often used in 3D object detection to capture spatial information.

Graph-based approaches, like Graph Convolutional Networks (GCNs), are employed for 3D object detection tasks, leveraging the relationships between points or voxels in a point cloud.

In video object detection, temporal information is crucial for tracking objects across frames. Recurrent Neural Networks (RNNs) and Long Short-Term Memory (LSTM) networks are integrated into detection models to maintain object identity over time.

Object detection techniques continue to evolve, with ongoing research focused on improving accuracy, speed, and robustness. Efforts to handle occlusions, scale variations, and complex scenes are ongoing.

Semi-supervised and self-supervised learning approaches aim to reduce the reliance on large labeled datasets, making object detection more accessible for new domains and applications.

Real-time object detection on edge devices, such as smartphones and embedded systems, is a growing area of interest, requiring lightweight and efficient models.

In summary, object detection techniques have made remarkable progress in recent years, driven by advancements in deep learning and the availability of large datasets. These techniques have a wide range of applications, from traditional image and video analysis to emerging fields like autonomous robotics and augmented reality.

As technology continues to advance, object detection will play an increasingly critical role in our daily lives, enhancing the capabilities of machines and enabling new possibilities in various domains.

Localization and bounding box prediction are fundamental tasks in object detection, allowing machines to not only recognize objects but also precisely locate them within an image. These tasks are critical for various applications, including autonomous vehicles, robotics, and augmented reality.

Bounding box prediction involves identifying the coordinates that define the rectangle encompassing an object's location. The goal is to determine the box's top-left and bottom-right corners or its center coordinates, width, and height.

In object detection, each detected object is associated with a bounding box that tightly encloses it. The accuracy of bounding box predictions is essential for the correct localization and identification of objects.

One approach to bounding box prediction is to treat it as a regression problem, where the network learns to predict the offsets from a predefined anchor box. The anchor box is a reference box with a fixed aspect ratio and size, used as a template for predicting the final bounding box.

Regression-based methods use a convolutional neural network (CNN) to extract features from the entire image or region of interest. These features are then used to predict the bounding box's coordinates and dimensions.

Bounding box prediction is often combined with object classification in a two-stage process. In the first stage, the network generates multiple region proposals, which are potential object locations. These proposals are refined in the second stage, where the network predicts the bounding boxes and class probabilities for each proposal.

Region-based CNNs (R-CNNs) and their successors, such as Fast R-CNN and Faster R-CNN, adopt this two-stage approach. They employ region proposal networks (RPNs) to generate region proposals, and then they refine the proposals using CNNs for classification and bounding box prediction.

Single-stage object detectors, like You Only Look Once (YOLO) and Single Shot MultiBox Detector (SSD), merge bounding box prediction and object classification into a single network. They divide the image into a grid of cells and predict bounding boxes and class probabilities for each cell.

YOLO, in particular, uses a direct regression approach to predict bounding box coordinates and class probabilities. It divides the image into a grid, and each cell predicts multiple bounding boxes and associated class probabilities.

SSD, on the other hand, employs multiple convolutional layers at different scales to predict bounding boxes, enabling the detection of objects at various sizes.

Anchor-based methods, like RetinaNet, utilize anchor boxes to handle objects of different sizes and aspect ratios. They predict the offsets and scales for each anchor box to generate final bounding boxes.

The choice between two-stage and single-stage detectors depends on the application's requirements. Two-stage detectors often provide higher accuracy but may be slower, while single-stage detectors are faster but may sacrifice some accuracy.

Bounding box prediction also faces challenges, such as handling objects of various scales, aspect ratios, and orientations. Some methods introduce anchor boxes with different characteristics to address these challenges.

Non-maximum suppression (NMS) is a post-processing technique commonly used to refine bounding box predictions. NMS removes redundant bounding boxes with overlapping areas, retaining only the most confident ones.

Bounding box prediction extends beyond 2D images to 3D object detection in point clouds and depth data. In 3D object detection, the goal is to predict 3D bounding boxes that enclose objects in the physical world.

LiDAR sensors, which measure distance using laser pulses, are often used in 3D object detection. Point cloud data from LiDAR sensors is processed to identify objects and estimate their 3D positions and orientations.

Graph-based methods, like Graph Convolutional Networks (GCNs), are applied to point cloud data to predict 3D bounding boxes. GCNs capture relationships between points in the point cloud, aiding in accurate localization.

Bounding box prediction is not limited to static objects but also applies to object tracking in videos. In video object tracking, bounding boxes are predicted for objects across frames to maintain their identities.

Recurrent Neural Networks (RNNs) and Long Short-Term Memory (LSTM) networks are used in video object tracking to maintain object identities and predict bounding boxes over time.

Bounding box prediction techniques continue to advance, with ongoing research focusing on improving accuracy, handling occlusions, and addressing complex scenarios. Methods that fuse information from multiple sensors, such as cameras, LiDAR, and radar, are becoming increasingly important for robust object localization.

In summary, localization and bounding box prediction are essential components of object detection, enabling machines to not only recognize objects but also precisely locate them within images or in the physical world. These tasks are crucial for a wide range of applications, from autonomous vehicles and robotics to augmented reality and surveillance systems.

As technology continues to advance, bounding box prediction techniques will play a pivotal role in enhancing the capabilities of machines and enabling new possibilities in various domains.

Chapter 5: Semantic Segmentation and Instance Segmentation

Semantic segmentation is a computer vision task that takes object detection a step further by assigning a class label to every pixel in an image. It involves pixel-level classification, where each pixel is categorized into a specific object class or category.

Unlike object detection, which identifies and outlines objects with bounding boxes, semantic segmentation provides a detailed understanding of an image's content by segmenting it into regions corresponding to different object categories. This fine-grained segmentation is valuable for applications like scene understanding, autonomous navigation, and medical image analysis.

Semantic segmentation can be seen as an image-to-image mapping problem, where the input is an image, and the output is a pixel-wise class label map. The class label map assigns a unique category to each pixel, distinguishing between different objects and regions in the image.

Convolutional Neural Networks (CNNs) have played a pivotal role in advancing semantic segmentation. CNNs are well-suited for this task because they can capture local and global features while preserving spatial relationships.

Fully Convolutional Networks (FCNs) were among the early architectures specifically designed for semantic segmentation. FCNs replace fully connected layers with convolutional layers, allowing the network to process input images of arbitrary sizes and produce output feature maps of the same size.

FCNs upsample the feature maps to match the input image's dimensions, resulting in pixel-wise class predictions. These predictions are achieved through transposed convolutions or bilinear upsampling, followed by a softmax activation to obtain class probabilities.

Another popular architecture for semantic segmentation is the U-Net, which combines a contracting path to capture context with an expansive path for precise localization. U-Nets are widely used in medical image segmentation tasks due to their ability to handle limited data and produce accurate results.

DeepLab is a semantic segmentation architecture that incorporates atrous (dilated) convolutions to capture multi-scale context. This enables DeepLab to handle objects of various sizes and provide fine-grained segmentation.

Recent advancements in semantic segmentation have introduced methods like Mask R-CNN, which extends the Faster R-CNN object detection framework to include pixel-level instance segmentation. Mask R-CNN is capable of distinguishing between different instances of the same object category, providing pixel-wise masks for each instance.

Deeplabv3+ is an evolution of the DeepLab architecture that combines spatial pyramid pooling with an encoder-decoder structure. This architecture excels in capturing fine details and has achieved state-of-the-art performance on several semantic segmentation benchmarks.

One of the challenges in semantic segmentation is handling class imbalance, as some classes may be less frequent than others. To address this, techniques like class weighting or focal loss are used to assign different importance to each class during training.

Data augmentation is crucial in semantic segmentation to increase the diversity of training samples. Common augmentations include random scaling, cropping, flipping, and color jittering, which help the model generalize better to different scenarios.

Evaluation metrics for semantic segmentation include Intersection over Union (IoU), also known as the Jaccard Index, and pixel accuracy. IoU measures the overlap between the predicted and ground truth masks, while pixel accuracy quantifies the percentage of correctly classified pixels.

Semantic segmentation extends beyond 2D images to 3D point clouds and volumetric data. In medical imaging, for example, 3D semantic segmentation is used for organ and tumor delineation in 3D CT or MRI scans.

Graph-based approaches, such as Graph Convolutional Networks (GCNs), are applied to 3D point clouds to perform semantic segmentation by considering point relationships and local structures.

Real-time semantic segmentation on embedded devices is a growing area of interest. Efficient architectures and model quantization techniques are applied to meet the computational constraints of edge devices.

Semantic segmentation can also benefit from the fusion of multiple sensor modalities, such as cameras, LiDAR, and radar, for robust scene understanding. This fusion enhances perception systems in autonomous vehicles and robotics.

In summary, semantic segmentation is a crucial computer vision task that provides pixel-level classification, enabling machines to understand images at a fine-grained level. Convolutional Neural Networks have driven significant progress in semantic segmentation, with architectures like FCNs, U-Nets, DeepLab, and Mask R-CNN leading the way.

Handling class imbalance and data augmentation are essential considerations in semantic segmentation, and evaluation metrics like IoU and pixel accuracy help assess model performance. Semantic segmentation extends to 3D data and real-time edge computing, making it applicable to various domains, including medical imaging, autonomous vehicles, and robotics.

As technology continues to advance, semantic segmentation will continue to play a pivotal role in enhancing scene understanding and enabling new possibilities in computer vision applications.

Instance segmentation is a challenging computer vision task that builds upon the foundations of object detection and semantic segmentation. It aims to identify and distinguish individual instances of objects within an image, providing a pixel-wise segmentation where each object instance is assigned a unique label.

Unlike semantic segmentation, which assigns the same class label to all pixels belonging to the same object category, instance segmentation goes further by separating objects of the same category into distinct instances. This fine-grained segmentation is essential in applications such as autonomous driving, robotics, and interactive systems.

Instance segmentation can be considered as an extension of object detection, where in addition to locating objects, the task involves precisely delineating each object's boundaries at the pixel level. This level of detail is valuable for tasks that require interaction or manipulation of objects in the scene.

One approach to instance segmentation is to build upon the success of object detection frameworks like Faster R-CNN and Mask R-CNN. Mask R-CNN, in particular, extends Faster R-CNN to predict not only bounding boxes and class labels but also pixel-wise masks for each object instance.

Mask R-CNN operates in two stages: in the first stage, it generates region proposals, similar to Faster R-CNN, and in the second stage, it refines these proposals by predicting both class labels and instance-specific masks.

The mask prediction is achieved through a mask head, which is a small network applied to each region of interest (RoI) to produce binary masks that indicate the presence or absence of an object instance in each pixel.

An instance-aware loss function is used to train Mask R-CNN, ensuring that each instance mask is accurately predicted. This loss function combines binary cross-entropy for mask prediction and a classification loss for object detection.

Another architecture for instance segmentation is the Panoptic FPN, which combines semantic segmentation and instance segmentation in a single network. Panoptic FPN simultaneously predicts semantic segmentation maps and instance masks, providing both class-level and instance-level information.

The MaskLab architecture extends instance segmentation to multiple tasks, including instance-wise contour detection and fine-grained instance recognition. MaskLab's contour branch predicts object contours, enabling precise boundary delineation.

Instance segmentation faces challenges related to object occlusions, size variations, and complex scenes with multiple overlapping objects. Handling these challenges requires robust techniques for object separation and mask refinement.

One way to address object occlusions is through the use of non-maximum suppression (NMS) and post-processing techniques. NMS helps remove redundant overlapping object proposals, and mask refinement techniques refine the predicted masks to eliminate artifacts.

Data augmentation is crucial in instance segmentation to increase the diversity of training samples and improve model generalization. Augmentation techniques include random scaling, rotation, flipping, and color jittering.

Evaluating instance segmentation models involves metrics such as mean Average Precision (mAP) and mask Average Precision (mask AP). These metrics assess the accuracy of both object detection and instance mask prediction.

Instance segmentation extends beyond 2D images to 3D point clouds and volumetric data. In 3D instance segmentation, the goal is to segment and distinguish individual objects within 3D scenes, often captured by LiDAR sensors or depth cameras.

Graph-based approaches, such as Graph Convolutional Networks (GCNs), are applied to point cloud data for 3D instance segmentation. GCNs capture relationships between points and enable precise separation of objects in 3D space.

Instance segmentation is a computationally intensive task, and optimizing model inference speed is crucial for real-time applications. Efficient architectures and hardware acceleration techniques are employed to meet real-time requirements.

In summary, instance segmentation is a challenging computer vision task that combines object detection with fine-grained pixel-level segmentation. Frameworks like Mask R-CNN and Panoptic FPN have significantly advanced instance segmentation, enabling machines to identify and distinguish individual object instances within images.

Handling occlusions, variations in object size, and complex scenes are ongoing challenges in instance segmentation. Data augmentation and evaluation metrics such as mAP and mask AP play vital roles in model development and assessment.

Instance segmentation extends to 3D data and real-time applications, making it applicable to various domains, including robotics, autonomous driving, and interactive systems.

As technology continues to advance, instance segmentation will continue to play a pivotal role in enhancing scene understanding and enabling new possibilities in computer vision applications.

Chapter 6: Face Recognition and Biometric Applications

Face recognition is a complex and fascinating field within computer vision that involves identifying and verifying individuals based on their facial features. While it has made significant advancements in recent years, it still faces unique challenges that make it an ongoing area of research and development.

One of the primary challenges in face recognition is handling variations in lighting conditions. Faces can appear differently under various lighting conditions, which can affect the appearance of key facial features. This is particularly challenging in real-world scenarios where lighting can be unpredictable.

Another significant challenge is pose variation. Faces can be seen from different angles and orientations, which can make it challenging to align and match facial features accurately. Dealing with variations in pose is essential for robust face recognition systems.

Face recognition systems also need to address changes in facial expressions. People often exhibit a range of expressions, from smiling to frowning, which can alter the appearance of their faces. Recognizing individuals across different expressions is crucial for practical applications.

A critical challenge is handling occlusions, where parts of a person's face are partially or fully covered. This can occur due to accessories like glasses or scarves or even by the person's hand. Occlusions can significantly hinder face recognition accuracy.

Age progression and regression are additional challenges. As people age, their facial features can change gradually, impacting the performance of face recognition systems designed for specific age groups. Accurate recognition across different age groups is important, especially in applications like age verification.

Ethnicity and race diversity pose unique challenges in face recognition. Facial features can vary significantly among different ethnic groups, making it essential to build inclusive and unbiased face recognition systems.

The presence of makeup, tattoos, or facial hair can also affect the appearance of a person's face. These alterations need to be accounted for in face recognition algorithms to ensure accurate results.

One of the most critical challenges in face recognition is privacy and ethical concerns. The use of face recognition technology in surveillance and public spaces has raised questions about individual privacy and surveillance. Balancing the benefits of face recognition with privacy and ethical considerations is an ongoing challenge.

The issue of data bias is significant in face recognition. Many face recognition algorithms are trained on biased datasets, leading to disparities in performance across different demographics. Efforts to address data bias and create more diverse training datasets are essential.

Security is another challenge in face recognition, particularly for applications like facial authentication. Ensuring that face recognition systems are robust against spoofing attempts, such as using photos or masks to impersonate someone, is crucial.

Scalability is a challenge when deploying face recognition in large-scale applications. Efficient algorithms and hardware acceleration are needed to handle a high volume of face recognition requests in real-time.

Face recognition must also consider factors like resolution and image quality. Low-resolution or noisy images can make it difficult to extract accurate facial features and match faces correctly.

In addition to 2D face recognition, there is a growing interest in 3D face recognition, which leverages depth information to improve accuracy. 3D face recognition can handle variations in pose and is less affected by changes in lighting.

Face recognition systems need to ensure user consent and data protection. Clear policies and guidelines should be established to govern the collection, storage, and use of facial data.

Interoperability is a challenge in face recognition systems. Ensuring that different systems and devices can work together seamlessly is essential for widespread adoption.

The unique challenges of face recognition have led to ongoing research in areas such as deep learning, multi-modal fusion (combining data from different sensors), and domain adaptation (adapting algorithms to different environments). These efforts aim to improve the robustness, accuracy, and fairness of face recognition systems.

Despite the challenges, face recognition has made significant progress and has a wide range of applications, from unlocking smartphones to enhancing security and facilitating personalized experiences.

As technology continues to evolve, addressing the unique challenges of face recognition will be crucial for its responsible and ethical use in society.

Biometric applications extend far beyond the realm of face recognition, encompassing a diverse range of technologies and use cases. Biometrics, which involves the measurement and analysis of unique physical or behavioral characteristics, has found applications in various fields due to its reliability and security.

One notable application of biometrics is fingerprint recognition, which is one of the oldest and most widely used biometric technologies. Fingerprints are unique to each individual, and their patterns can be captured and matched with high accuracy. This technology is commonly used for identity verification and access control, such as unlocking smartphones and securing sensitive areas.

Iris recognition is another biometric technology that has gained popularity in recent years. The iris, the colored part of the eye, contains unique patterns that can be captured and used for identification. Iris recognition is known for its high accuracy and is used in applications like border control and access management at secure facilities.

Voice recognition, also known as speaker recognition, is a behavioral biometric technology that analyzes an individual's voice patterns. Voiceprints, which include factors like pitch, tone, and speech cadence, are used to verify a person's identity. Voice recognition is commonly used in call centers for user authentication and in voice assistants for personalized interactions.

Hand geometry recognition is a biometric technology that captures the size and shape of a person's hand. This method is often used for access control in workplaces and can also be integrated with time and attendance systems.

Signature recognition, which analyzes a person's handwritten signature, is widely used for financial transactions and document authentication. It is commonly used in banking and legal sectors to verify the authenticity of signatures on checks and contracts.

Vein recognition is a relatively newer biometric technology that scans the patterns of veins beneath the skin's surface, typically in the palm or finger. Vein recognition offers a high level of security and is used in applications like access control and secure authentication.

Gait analysis, a behavioral biometric technology, focuses on an individual's walking pattern. It analyzes factors like stride length and rhythm to identify a person. Gait analysis has applications in security and surveillance, especially in scenarios where other biometrics may not be feasible.

DNA fingerprinting, although not used for real-time authentication, is a powerful biometric technology for forensic and paternity testing. It analyzes specific regions of an individual's DNA to establish identity or biological relationships.

Ear recognition, which analyzes the shape and features of a person's ear, is used in some security and access control applications. Earprints are unique to individuals and can be used for identification.

Palmprint recognition, similar to fingerprint recognition, analyzes the unique patterns on the palm of a person's hand. It is used in various access control and identity verification applications.

Behavioral biometrics, such as keystroke dynamics and mouse movement analysis, focus on an individual's behavior while interacting with digital devices. These biometrics can be used for continuous authentication and fraud detection in online systems.

Biometric applications extend beyond individual recognition and access control to broader security and surveillance purposes. Biometric systems are used in law enforcement for criminal identification and tracking, such as fingerprint matching and facial recognition in security cameras.

Biometrics also play a crucial role in healthcare, with applications like patient identification, access to medical records, and medication dispensing. Biometric systems help enhance patient safety and reduce medical errors.

In the financial sector, biometric authentication is increasingly used for secure transactions and fraud prevention. Fingerprint or facial recognition can be used to authorize financial transactions on mobile devices.

Biometric applications have made their way into travel and border control, with biometric passports and eGates that use facial or iris recognition to streamline immigration processes. Biometrics are not limited to authentication; they also contribute to improving user experiences. For example, smart homes and IoT devices use voice recognition to provide personalized and convenient interactions with users. Biometric applications raise important ethical and privacy considerations. Issues related to data protection, consent, and misuse of biometric data require careful consideration and regulation. Balancing the benefits of biometrics with privacy and security concerns is an ongoing challenge.

Advancements in machine learning and deep learning have contributed to the accuracy and reliability of biometric systems. These technologies continue to drive innovation in biometric applications, making them more accessible and applicable in various domains.

As technology evolves, biometric applications will likely continue to expand, offering new ways to enhance security, streamline processes, and improve user experiences.

In summary, biometric technologies extend far beyond face recognition and offer a wide range of applications in security, access control, healthcare, finance, and more. Their unique ability to provide reliable and secure identification makes them valuable tools in a rapidly evolving digital world. However, the ethical and privacy considerations associated with biometric data collection and usage require careful attention and regulation to ensure responsible and ethical applications.

Chapter 7: Deep Learning for Image Generation and Style Transfer

Generative models for image synthesis represent a significant advancement in the field of computer vision and artificial intelligence. These models are capable of generating highly realistic and coherent images, often indistinguishable from photographs taken in the real world.

One of the most prominent types of generative models for image synthesis is the Generative Adversarial Network (GAN). GANs consist of two neural networks, a generator, and a discriminator, which are trained simultaneously in a competitive fashion. The generator generates fake images, while the discriminator evaluates the authenticity of those images.

During training, the generator's objective is to create images that are convincing enough to fool the discriminator, while the discriminator's objective is to become increasingly proficient at distinguishing real from fake images. This adversarial training process leads to the generator producing high-quality, realistic images.

Conditional GANs are a variant of GANs that allow for the generation of images based on specific conditions or labels. For example, conditional GANs can generate images of different animal species by conditioning on the desired label, making them highly versatile for various image synthesis tasks.

Another popular type of generative model is the Variational Autoencoder (VAE). VAEs are probabilistic models that learn to generate data by modeling the underlying probability distribution of the data. They consist of an encoder that maps data into a latent space and a decoder that generates data from samples in the latent space.

VAEs are particularly useful for image synthesis because they can generate new images by sampling from the learned latent space. This allows for the creation of diverse and novel images by interpolating between different latent space points.

VAEs also have the advantage of being interpretable, as the latent space often corresponds to meaningful features of the data, such as object shapes or styles. This interpretability makes VAEs valuable for tasks like image editing and style transfer.

The choice of architecture and training strategies plays a crucial role in the quality of generated images. Architectures like Deep Convolutional GANs (DCGANs) and Progressive GANs have been developed to improve the stability and quality of image synthesis.

Progressive GANs, for example, start with generating low-resolution images and progressively increase the resolution during training. This approach results in sharper and more realistic images.

Style-based generators, such as those used in StyleGAN and StyleGAN2, allow for explicit control over the style and appearance of generated images. Users can manipulate factors like age, gender, and expression to generate highly customizable images.

Image-to-image translation is another application of generative models. These models learn to convert images from one domain to another while preserving important characteristics. For example, they can transform sketches into realistic images or change the weather in a photo.

CycleGAN is a notable example of an image-to-image translation model that can perform tasks like turning photos into artworks or converting images from summer to winter.

Super-resolution is another image synthesis task where generative models excel. These models enhance the quality of low-resolution images by generating high-resolution counterparts. This is useful in applications like upscaling old movies or improving the quality of medical images.

The generation of photorealistic human faces is a challenging task that has seen significant progress with generative models. Models like StyleGAN2 can synthesize highly detailed and believable portraits, contributing to advancements in computer graphics and virtual characters.

Artistic style transfer is a creative application of generative models that allows users to apply the artistic style of one image to the content of another. This has resulted in the creation of stunning visual effects and artistic compositions.

Generative models have practical applications in data augmentation for training machine learning models. By generating additional training data, these models can improve the performance and robustness of various machine learning tasks.

Generative models for image synthesis have also raised ethical concerns related to the generation of fake or misleading content, often referred to as deepfakes. These concerns underscore the importance of responsible and ethical use of generative technology. In summary, generative models for image synthesis represent a remarkable achievement in the field of computer vision. They have enabled the generation of highly realistic and diverse images across various domains, from photorealistic human faces to artistic compositions.

These models continue to evolve, with ongoing research in architecture design, training strategies, and applications. Their impact spans from creative expression to practical data augmentation, making them a significant driver of innovation in computer vision and artificial intelligence.

As generative models advance, it is crucial to address ethical concerns and ensure responsible usage to benefit society while mitigating potential risks.

Artistic style transfer with deep learning is a fascinating application of neural networks that allows for the transformation of images into unique artistic styles. This technology has gained popularity for its ability to combine the content of one image with the artistic style of another, resulting in visually striking compositions.

The concept of style transfer can be traced back to artistic endeavors, where painters and artists have long sought to blend different styles to create innovative works. With the advent of deep learning, this artistic process has been automated and made accessible to a broader audience.

One of the key techniques used for artistic style transfer is the Convolutional Neural Network (CNN). CNNs are a type of deep neural network that have demonstrated exceptional capabilities in image-related tasks, such as image recognition and segmentation.

In artistic style transfer, a CNN is employed to separate the content and style of an image. The content represents the underlying subject matter and structure, while the style captures the texture, colors, and brushwork of an artwork.

The process begins with selecting two input images: one for content and one for style. The content image serves as the basis for the composition, while the style image provides the desired artistic characteristics.

A pre-trained CNN, often based on architectures like VGG or ResNet, is used to extract feature maps from both the content and style images. These feature maps capture information about the content and style of each image.

To generate the stylized image, the content and style features are combined in a way that preserves the content structure while infusing the style characteristics. This is achieved through optimization techniques, typically involving gradient descent.

The objective is to minimize the difference between the stylized image and the content image in terms of content features and the difference between the stylized image and the style image in terms of style features. By finding the right balance between these objectives, the neural network generates a visually appealing stylized image.

Artistic style transfer is highly customizable, allowing users to control the degree of stylization. Parameters like the content-weight and style-weight can be adjusted to emphasize content or style in the final composition.

One of the early breakthroughs in artistic style transfer was achieved with the development of the Gatys et al. algorithm, often referred to as Neural Style Transfer. This algorithm introduced the concept of Gram matrices to capture style information and laid the foundation for subsequent advancements in the field.

Artistic style transfer has broad applications, ranging from transforming ordinary photos into artistic masterpieces to creating unique visual effects in movies and video games. It has also been used in the fashion industry for designing clothing patterns and textile prints.

One of the exciting aspects of artistic style transfer is the ability to explore different artistic styles and experiment with creativity. With the right input images and parameter settings, it is possible to generate a wide range of artistic outcomes, from Impressionist paintings to Cubist compositions.

To make artistic style transfer accessible to a broader audience, various software applications and online tools have been developed. These tools often provide user-friendly interfaces that allow individuals with limited technical expertise to apply style transfer to their images.

As with any technology, artistic style transfer also raises ethical considerations. The ease with which deep learning models can create convincing forgeries has led to concerns about the potential misuse of this technology, including the creation of deepfake images and videos.

Addressing these ethical concerns and ensuring responsible use of style transfer technology is essential as it continues to evolve and become more accessible.

In summary, artistic style transfer with deep learning is a powerful and creative application of neural networks. It allows for the fusion of content and style from different images, resulting in visually captivating compositions.

This technology has applications in diverse fields, from art and design to entertainment and fashion. As it becomes more accessible, it offers new possibilities for artistic expression and visual storytelling.

However, it is essential to approach style transfer with a responsible and ethical mindset, considering the potential consequences of its misuse.

Artistic style transfer is a testament to the synergy between art and technology, and its continued development promises to unlock even more creative potential in the future.

Chapter 8: 3D Computer Vision and Depth Estimation

Depth perception is a fundamental aspect of human vision that allows us to perceive the three-dimensional structure of the world around us. In computer vision, replicating this ability to estimate the depth or distance of objects from images and videos is a challenging and essential task.

The importance of depth perception in computer vision is evident in various applications. For instance, in autonomous driving, accurately estimating the depth of objects and obstacles is crucial for safe navigation and collision avoidance.

Depth perception also plays a significant role in augmented reality (AR) and virtual reality (VR) applications, where virtual objects need to be placed in the correct spatial context to create convincing experiences.

In robotics, robots equipped with depth perception capabilities can manipulate objects more effectively and navigate complex environments with precision.

One of the primary methods for depth perception in computer vision is stereopsis, which is inspired by human binocular vision. Stereopsis relies on the slight disparity or difference in the viewpoints of our left and right eyes to estimate the depth of objects.

To replicate this in computer vision, stereo cameras or pairs of cameras are used to capture images from slightly different perspectives. These images, referred to as stereo pairs, can then be processed to calculate the depth information by identifying corresponding points in the two images and measuring their disparity.

Depth from stereo vision, while effective, has limitations. It requires careful calibration of the stereo camera setup, and its accuracy can be affected by factors like lighting conditions and the presence of texture on objects.

Another widely used method for depth perception is structured light. Structured light systems project known patterns onto objects, and the deformation of these patterns on the object's surface is used to infer depth information.

For example, a common structured light approach involves projecting a grid of laser lines onto an object. The deformation of the grid on the object's surface is captured by a camera and used to calculate depth.

Structured light systems are highly accurate and can provide dense depth maps, but they can be sensitive to environmental factors like ambient light and surface reflectivity.

Time-of-flight (ToF) cameras are another technology for depth perception. ToF cameras emit light signals and measure the time it takes for the light to bounce back from objects. By calculating the round-trip time, these cameras can estimate the distance to objects.

ToF cameras have become popular in consumer devices like gaming consoles and smartphones due to their speed and relatively low cost.

Another method for depth perception is monocular depth estimation, which involves estimating depth from a single camera image. This is a challenging task because it lacks the stereo or additional information provided by multiple cameras.

Monocular depth estimation often relies on machine learning techniques, such as deep neural networks. Convolutional neural networks (CNNs) have been particularly successful in this domain, learning to predict depth from large datasets of images with ground truth depth information.

Monocular depth estimation models can be trained on diverse datasets to handle various scenarios and environments. However, their accuracy can be influenced by factors like the availability of training data and the complexity of the scenes they encounter.

LiDAR (Light Detection and Ranging) is another technology used for depth perception, especially in autonomous vehicles and robotics. LiDAR systems emit laser beams and measure the time it takes for the light to return after hitting objects. By scanning laser beams in multiple directions, LiDAR sensors can generate detailed 3D point clouds of the environment.

LiDAR offers high accuracy and precision in depth estimation and is particularly robust in various lighting conditions. However, it can be expensive and bulky, limiting its use in some applications.

Stereo matching algorithms, which analyze stereo pairs of images to find corresponding points, have also seen advancements. These algorithms use techniques like disparity maps and graph cuts to estimate depth from images effectively.

Recent advancements in depth perception have been driven by the combination of deep learning and traditional computer vision techniques. Deep neural networks, especially convolutional neural networks (CNNs), have shown remarkable capabilities in monocular depth estimation and stereo matching.

Efforts to develop lightweight and efficient neural network architectures have made it possible to deploy depth perception models on resource-constrained devices, such as smartphones and drones.

In summary, depth perception is a critical aspect of computer vision that enables applications in fields like autonomous driving, augmented reality, robotics, and more.

Various methods, including stereo vision, structured light, time-of-flight cameras, monocular depth estimation, and LiDAR, are used to estimate depth information accurately.

Advancements in machine learning, particularly deep neural networks, have enhanced the accuracy and efficiency of depth perception algorithms. As technology continues to evolve, depth perception in computer vision will play an increasingly important role in enabling machines to perceive and interact with the 3D world.

Applications of 3D computer vision are diverse and span across various fields, demonstrating the profound impact this technology has on the way we interact with the world. One of the key domains where 3D computer vision plays a significant role is in autonomous robotics.

Robotic systems equipped with 3D vision capabilities can navigate complex environments more effectively, avoiding obstacles and making informed decisions based on their surroundings. This is crucial for applications like autonomous drones, self-driving cars, and industrial automation.

In the realm of healthcare, 3D computer vision has revolutionized medical imaging and diagnostics. Medical imaging techniques, such as MRI and CT scans, rely on 3D reconstruction to provide detailed insights into the human body's internal structures.

3D computer vision is also used in surgical planning and guidance, enabling surgeons to visualize complex anatomical structures and perform minimally invasive procedures with precision.

In the field of archaeology and cultural heritage preservation, 3D computer vision is used to digitize and preserve historical artifacts, monuments, and archaeological sites. By creating detailed 3D models, researchers can study and document these treasures for future generations.

Augmented reality (AR) and virtual reality (VR) applications heavily depend on 3D computer vision for creating immersive experiences. AR overlays virtual objects onto the real world, while VR places users in entirely virtual environments, both relying on accurate tracking of the user's surroundings.

In the entertainment industry, 3D computer vision is used to capture motion and facial expressions for animation and gaming. This technology enables the creation of lifelike characters and immersive gaming experiences.

In agriculture, 3D computer vision is employed for precision farming. Drones equipped with 3D vision sensors can assess crop health, monitor field conditions, and optimize irrigation and pesticide application.

The construction industry benefits from 3D computer vision by improving project planning and management. Construction sites use 3D modeling and monitoring to track progress, identify potential issues, and ensure safety compliance.

Retail and e-commerce companies employ 3D computer vision for various applications, including product recognition, inventory management, and augmented reality shopping experiences. Customers can visualize products in their own space before making purchase decisions.

3D computer vision also plays a critical role in the development of self-driving cars. These vehicles rely on a combination of sensors, including LiDAR and cameras, to perceive their environment in three dimensions and make real-time driving decisions.

In the field of geospatial analysis, 3D computer vision aids in cartography, environmental monitoring, and disaster management. It enables the creation of accurate 3D models of terrain and buildings for improved spatial analysis.

The manufacturing sector benefits from 3D computer vision for quality control and automation. Robotic systems equipped with 3D vision sensors can inspect products for defects and perform complex assembly tasks with precision.

3D computer vision is also used in the field of cultural heritage preservation, enabling the digitization and restoration of artworks, sculptures, and historical sites. This technology allows for the preservation of cultural treasures for future generations.

In the aerospace industry, 3D computer vision is employed for aircraft inspection and maintenance. Drones equipped with 3D sensors can inspect aircraft surfaces and structures, ensuring safety and reducing maintenance costs.

Furthermore, 3D computer vision is utilized in the field of agriculture for crop monitoring and yield estimation. Drones equipped with 3D sensors can capture data about crop health and growth, enabling farmers to make informed decisions and optimize their yields.

In the world of fashion and retail, 3D computer vision is transforming the way clothing and accessories are designed and sold. Virtual try-on applications allow customers to see how clothing items look and fit without trying them on physically.

3D computer vision is also making significant contributions to the field of urban planning and architecture. It enables the creation of accurate 3D models of cities and buildings, facilitating better urban design, transportation planning, and infrastructure development.

In summary, the applications of 3D computer vision are extensive and diverse, impacting fields ranging from healthcare and entertainment to agriculture and aerospace. This technology has the potential to revolutionize industries and improve the way we interact with the world around us.

As technology continues to advance, the capabilities of 3D computer vision will expand, opening up new possibilities and applications that we can only begin to imagine. The convergence of 3D computer vision with other emerging technologies, such as artificial intelligence and augmented reality, will further accelerate its adoption and transformational impact on society.

Chapter 9: Transfer Learning for Computer Vision

Leveraging pretrained models in computer vision is a powerful approach that has transformed the field by enabling the reuse of learned features and representations. These pretrained models, often based on deep neural networks, have been trained on large datasets for tasks like image classification, object detection, and image segmentation.

One of the primary benefits of using pretrained models is the ability to transfer knowledge from one task to another. Rather than training a neural network from scratch, researchers and practitioners can take advantage of the features and representations already learned by pretrained models.

This approach significantly reduces the computational resources and data required for training, making it feasible to achieve state-of-the-art results even with limited resources. In essence, pretrained models serve as a form of transfer learning, where knowledge gained from one task is applied to another task.

The ImageNet dataset, containing millions of labeled images across thousands of categories, has been instrumental in the development of pretrained models. Many popular pretrained models, such as the VGG series, ResNet, Inception, and MobileNet, have their roots in ImageNet-based training.

When leveraging pretrained models, one common practice is feature extraction. This involves using the layers of a pretrained model to extract high-level features from input images. These features can then be fed into another model, such as a classifier or regression network, to perform a specific task.

Feature extraction with pretrained models is particularly useful when dealing with limited labeled data. By using features learned from a large dataset, the model can generalize better to new data and perform well on tasks like image recognition or object detection.

Another approach is fine-tuning, where only a portion of the pretrained model is modified and retrained on a new dataset. Fine-tuning allows the model to adapt its learned representations to the specific characteristics of the target task.

For example, in transfer learning for image classification, the lower layers of a pretrained convolutional neural network (CNN) can capture general features like edges and textures. In contrast, the higher layers may encode more task-specific information, such as object shapes and categories.

Fine-tuning typically involves freezing the lower layers to retain their learned features and updating the higher layers to adapt to the new task. This process helps the model specialize in the target domain while benefiting from the general knowledge encoded in the pretrained model.

The choice of which layers to freeze and which to fine-tune depends on the similarity between the source and target tasks. For closely related tasks, fine-tuning more layers may be beneficial, while for dissimilar tasks, it's often preferable to freeze more layers to preserve the source task's knowledge.

Pretrained models have revolutionized computer vision applications. In image classification, for instance, models pretrained on large datasets like ImageNet have become the basis for achieving high accuracy. Researchers and practitioners can take these models, modify the output layer to match the target classes, and fine-tune them on their specific dataset.

Object detection is another area where pretrained models have made a significant impact. Models like Faster R-CNN and YOLO (You Only Look Once) leverage pretrained CNNs for feature extraction and then fine-tune their object detection heads for precise localization and recognition of objects in images.

Pretrained models have also been instrumental in advancing semantic segmentation, where each pixel in an image is assigned a class label. Models like U-Net and Mask R-CNN utilize pretrained encoders to capture image features and then decode them into pixel-wise segmentation masks.

Furthermore, pretrained models are employed in image captioning, where the goal is to generate textual descriptions of images. These models use their learned representations to understand image content and produce coherent and contextually relevant captions.

In the context of generative models, pretrained models like GPT (Generative Pretrained Transformer) have demonstrated remarkable capabilities in generating realistic and contextually coherent text. These models have been fine-tuned for various natural language processing tasks, including language translation and text summarization.

The availability of pretrained models has democratized the field of computer vision and natural language processing. Researchers and developers can access pretrained models and adapt them to their specific tasks with relative ease.

However, it's important to consider the ethical implications of using pretrained models. Bias and fairness concerns can arise from the data used to train these models, and practitioners must be vigilant in addressing and mitigating potential biases in their applications.

Moreover, as the use of pretrained models becomes more prevalent, it is crucial to continue research and development efforts to improve their robustness, efficiency, and adaptability to various domains and tasks.

In summary, leveraging pretrained models in computer vision and natural language processing has revolutionized the way we approach and solve complex tasks. These models, initially trained on large and diverse datasets, provide a valuable foundation for transfer learning, enabling the development of state-of-the-art solutions with fewer resources and less data.

The versatility of pretrained models extends to various computer vision tasks, including image classification, object detection, semantic segmentation, and image captioning, as well as natural language processing tasks like language translation and text generation.

However, the responsible use of pretrained models requires careful consideration of potential biases and ethical concerns. As technology continues to advance, the integration of pretrained models into diverse applications will continue to drive innovation and broaden the horizons of what is achievable in the fields of computer vision and natural language understanding.

Fine-tuning and transfer learning strategies are essential techniques in machine learning and deep learning that enable models to leverage knowledge gained from one task and apply it to another. These strategies are particularly valuable when working with limited data or computational resources.

Fine-tuning involves taking a pre-existing model, often pretrained on a large dataset, and adapting it to a specific task or domain. This process typically focuses on adjusting the model's top layers while keeping the lower layers, responsible for feature extraction, frozen.

By doing so, the model can retain the knowledge it has acquired during the initial training phase while learning task-specific information in the top layers. This approach is beneficial in scenarios where the source and target tasks share some similarities.

One common example of fine-tuning is using a pretrained convolutional neural network (CNN) for image classification. The lower layers of the CNN capture general features like edges and textures, which are useful across a wide range of image-related tasks. The higher layers, on the other hand, encode more specific information about object shapes and categories.

In fine-tuning for a new image classification task, the lower layers remain unchanged to preserve their ability to recognize general features, while the final classification layer is modified to match the number of target classes. The model is then trained on the new dataset, adapting its high-level features to the specific classification task.

Fine-tuning is not limited to image-related tasks; it can be applied to various domains, including natural language processing (NLP). In NLP, models pretrained on massive text corpora can be fine-tuned for tasks like sentiment analysis, text classification, or language translation.

Another transfer learning strategy is feature extraction, where a pretrained model's intermediate layers are used as feature extractors. These extracted features are then fed into another model, such as a classifier or regressor, for the target task.

Feature extraction is valuable when you want to leverage the general representations learned by a pretrained model but need to apply them to a different type of model or task. For instance, you can use a pretrained convolutional neural network (CNN) to extract image features and then use those features as input to a support vector machine (SVM) for classification.

Transfer learning and fine-tuning strategies are not limited to image and text tasks. They can be applied to various machine learning and deep learning problems, including speech recognition, recommendation systems, and reinforcement learning.

One of the challenges in transfer learning is selecting the right pretrained model and deciding how many layers to fine-tune. The choice of the source model should consider the similarity between the source and target tasks.

For instance, if you have a pretrained model for object recognition and want to use it for a related task like object detection, the source model is likely a good fit. However, if the tasks are significantly different, you may need to experiment with different source models or architectures.

The decision of which layers to fine-tune depends on the target task and the amount of available data. In some cases, fine-tuning only the final layers may be sufficient, while in others, fine-tuning several layers, or even all layers, may be necessary to adapt the model effectively.

The success of transfer learning and fine-tuning strategies depends on the availability of a suitable pretrained model and a high-quality target dataset. Collecting and curating the right data for the target task is crucial for achieving good performance.

Another important consideration is domain adaptation, where the source and target domains differ significantly. In such cases, techniques like domain adaptation or domain adversarial training can help bridge the gap between the two domains.

It's worth noting that pretrained models and transfer learning strategies have democratized the field of machine learning. Researchers and developers can take advantage of existing models and adapt them to their specific tasks with less effort and computational resources.

This approach has led to remarkable progress in various fields and applications, including computer vision, natural language processing, and speech recognition.

Furthermore, pretrained models have opened up opportunities for developers and organizations with limited access to large datasets or computational power. These models serve as a valuable starting point for building effective machine learning solutions.

However, it's essential to be aware of potential biases and limitations present in pretrained models. The data used to train these models may introduce biases that can affect their behavior in downstream applications. It's crucial to evaluate and, if necessary, retrain the models on representative datasets to address bias and fairness concerns.

In summary, fine-tuning and transfer learning strategies are powerful techniques that enable the reuse of knowledge gained from one task to improve performance on another. These strategies are particularly valuable when working with limited data or computational resources.

Fine-tuning involves adapting a pretrained model to a specific task by modifying its top layers while keeping the lower layers frozen. Feature extraction leverages the intermediate layers of a pretrained model as feature extractors for another model.

Selecting the right source model, deciding which layers to fine-tune, and curating high-quality target data are crucial considerations for successful transfer learning. Pretrained models and transfer learning strategies have democratized the field of machine learning, making it more accessible and enabling rapid progress in various applications.

However, it's important to be mindful of potential biases and limitations in pretrained models and to address them responsibly in applications to ensure fairness and robustness.

Chapter 10: Advanced Topics in Computer Vision and Emerging Trends

Cutting-edge techniques in computer vision are at the forefront of technological advancements and are shaping the future of how we perceive, interact with, and understand the visual world. These techniques encompass a wide range of innovative approaches and methodologies that push the boundaries of what's possible in computer vision.

One of the most notable trends in cutting-edge computer vision is the use of deep learning models. Deep neural networks, particularly convolutional neural networks (CNNs), have revolutionized image understanding and recognition tasks. The ability of deep learning models to learn hierarchical features directly from raw data has resulted in unprecedented accuracy in tasks like image classification and object detection.

Moreover, deep learning architectures have extended beyond traditional 2D image analysis to tackle 3D vision problems. Researchers have developed novel techniques to process and interpret 3D data, such as point clouds and depth maps, enabling applications in robotics, augmented reality, and autonomous navigation.

Generative Adversarial Networks (GANs) and Variational Autoencoders (VAEs) are another cutting-edge area of computer vision. GANs, in particular, have gained immense popularity for generating realistic and high-quality images. They work by training two neural networks, a generator and a discriminator, in a competitive process that results in the generation of convincing synthetic data.

The use of GANs extends beyond image generation. Researchers have applied GANs for tasks like super-resolution, style transfer, and even generating photorealistic images from textual descriptions.

In addition to GANs, VAEs have shown promise in generating novel data samples. These models focus on encoding data into a latent space and then decoding it to produce samples that resemble the input data distribution. VAEs have been used in applications like image inpainting, where missing parts of an image are filled in with plausible content.

Attention mechanisms and transformer architectures have gained prominence in computer vision, particularly for tasks involving sequential data and long-range dependencies. Transformers, initially developed for natural language processing, have been adapted to vision tasks with remarkable success. They have demonstrated the ability to capture contextual information across large image regions, improving tasks like image captioning and object tracking.

In the realm of object detection, one of the cutting-edge techniques is the development of single-stage detectors like YOLO (You Only Look Once) and EfficientDet. These models achieve real-time or near-real-time performance while maintaining high accuracy in object localization and recognition. Their efficiency makes them suitable for applications like autonomous driving and surveillance.

Another significant advancement in computer vision is the fusion of vision and language. Models like Visual Question Answering (VQA) systems can answer questions about images, while image captioning models generate natural language descriptions of visual content. These techniques have applications in human-computer interaction, accessibility, and content understanding.

Continual learning and lifelong learning are becoming crucial in computer vision to address the challenge of model forgetting. As models are trained on new data, they risk losing knowledge of previously seen classes. Continual learning techniques aim to mitigate this issue by allowing models to adapt to new data while preserving knowledge from past experiences.

Robustness and interpretability are also critical in cutting-edge computer vision. Adversarial attacks, where small perturbations to an image can lead to misclassification, highlight the need for robust models. Research in adversarial defense and model interpretability is ongoing to ensure the reliability and transparency of computer vision systems.

Domain adaptation and transfer learning remain active research areas. Models trained on one domain or dataset often struggle when applied to a different domain or dataset. Developing techniques that can adapt models to new domains or fine-tune them for specific tasks without extensive data labeling is a challenge that continues to drive innovation.

Ethical considerations and fairness are increasingly important in computer vision research and application. Ensuring that computer vision systems do not exhibit biases, particularly gender, racial, or cultural biases, is a priority. Researchers and practitioners are working to develop fair and unbiased algorithms and evaluation metrics to promote ethical use of computer vision technology.

Cutting-edge computer vision techniques are also making a significant impact in healthcare. Applications range from medical image analysis and disease diagnosis to drug discovery and personalized medicine. Deep learning models have shown promise in identifying abnormalities in medical images, predicting patient outcomes, and accelerating the drug development process.

Additionally, computer vision has a growing role in environmental monitoring and conservation. Remote sensing technologies and satellite imagery are used to track changes in ecosystems, monitor wildlife populations, and assess the impact of climate change.

The integration of computer vision with robotics is leading to advancements in automation and autonomous systems. Robots equipped with vision sensors can navigate and interact with complex environments, perform tasks in unstructured settings, and collaborate with humans in various domains, including manufacturing, agriculture, and healthcare.

In the automotive industry, computer vision plays a crucial role in the development of self-driving cars. Vision sensors, such as cameras and LiDAR, enable vehicles to perceive their surroundings, identify objects, and make real-time driving decisions. This technology has the potential to revolutionize transportation and reduce accidents.

In summary, cutting-edge techniques in computer vision are shaping the future of technology and human interaction with the visual world. From deep learning and GANs to attention mechanisms, object detection, and domain adaptation, these techniques drive innovation in a wide range of applications, including healthcare, environmental monitoring, robotics, and autonomous systems.

Addressing ethical considerations, robustness, and interpretability is essential to ensure that computer vision technology benefits society while mitigating potential biases and challenges. As technology continues to evolve, computer vision will continue to push the boundaries of what is possible, unlocking new opportunities and applications that we have yet to imagine.

Emerging trends and future directions in the field of computer vision are driven by rapid technological advancements, evolving user demands, and novel applications across various industries. These trends provide a glimpse into the exciting possibilities that lie ahead, shaping the future of computer vision research and development.

One of the prominent emerging trends is the fusion of computer vision with other modalities, such as natural language processing (NLP) and robotics. Integrating vision with language understanding enables more sophisticated human-computer interactions, facilitating applications like visually grounded language generation and intelligent virtual assistants.

Moreover, combining computer vision with robotics leads to advancements in perception and control. Robots equipped with vision sensors can navigate complex environments, recognize objects, and interact with humans, enabling tasks in domains like healthcare, manufacturing, and autonomous vehicles.

In healthcare, computer vision is poised to play an increasingly vital role. Medical imaging, including techniques like MRI, CT, and X-ray, benefits from computer vision algorithms for faster diagnosis and disease detection. Additionally, wearable devices and smartphone apps with computer vision capabilities can monitor vital signs, assess skin conditions, and support telemedicine.

Real-time and low-latency computer vision applications are becoming more prevalent. These applications require fast processing and decision-making, making edge computing and efficient algorithms critical. For example, augmented reality (AR) and virtual reality (VR) applications demand real-time object recognition and tracking for immersive experiences.

Edge AI, which involves deploying machine learning models directly on devices, is a growing trend. This approach reduces reliance on cloud servers and enhances privacy. Cameras, drones, and IoT devices benefit from embedded computer vision capabilities for tasks like object detection, surveillance, and smart home automation.

Semantic segmentation, which assigns class labels to each pixel in an image, is gaining importance. It has applications in autonomous driving, where precise scene understanding is crucial for safe navigation. Furthermore, semantic segmentation aids in robotics for tasks like robotic surgery and warehouse automation.

Continual learning and lifelong learning techniques are vital for computer vision models to adapt to evolving environments and tasks. Developing algorithms that can acquire new knowledge while preserving previously learned information is a significant research direction.

Interdisciplinary collaborations are becoming more common in computer vision research. Collaborations with fields like neuroscience, cognitive science, and psychology provide insights into human perception, leading to more biologically inspired computer vision models. Understanding how the human brain processes visual information can lead to breakthroughs in artificial vision.

The integration of computer vision and natural language processing is not limited to text-based interactions. Visual question answering (VQA) and image captioning models enable AI systems to answer questions about images and generate descriptive sentences. These capabilities enhance human-computer communication and support visually impaired individuals.

Ethical considerations are increasingly prominent in computer vision research and applications. Addressing biases in data and algorithms, ensuring fairness, and promoting transparency are critical. Ethical guidelines and standards are being developed to guide responsible AI development and deployment.

Privacy-preserving computer vision techniques are essential in an era of increasing surveillance. Privacy-focused algorithms, such as federated learning and differential privacy, protect individuals' data while enabling broader applications in areas like smart cities and public safety.

The democratization of computer vision through open-source libraries, pre-trained models, and user-friendly development tools continues to empower researchers and developers worldwide. This accessibility accelerates innovation and expands the reach of computer vision technology.

The evolution of hardware, including specialized AI chips and GPUs, enables faster and more energy-efficient computer vision computations. These advancements are crucial for real-time applications, mobile devices, and edge computing.

Quantum computing holds the potential to revolutionize computer vision by solving complex optimization problems faster than classical computers. Although quantum computing is still in its infancy, it has the potential to accelerate research in areas like image reconstruction and computer vision algorithms.

The exploration of explainable AI (XAI) in computer vision is essential for building trust in AI systems. Interpretable models and techniques that provide insight into the decision-making process of AI algorithms are gaining importance.

Human-centric computer vision aims to enhance human experiences and well-being. Applications like emotion recognition, gesture-based interfaces, and personalized content recommendation leverage computer vision to create more empathetic and user-friendly technologies.

The intersection of computer vision with environmental science and sustainability is an emerging trend. Remote sensing and image analysis are used to monitor climate change, deforestation, wildlife conservation, and disaster management.

In summary, emerging trends and future directions in computer vision are driven by the fusion of vision with other modalities, real-time and low-latency applications, edge AI, semantic segmentation, continual learning, interdisciplinary collaborations, ethics, privacy, democratization, hardware advancements, quantum computing, explainable AI, human-centric applications, and environmental monitoring.

These trends are shaping the future of computer vision, offering exciting opportunities for research and development that will impact a wide range of industries and enhance our daily lives. As technology continues to evolve, the field of computer vision will continue to push the boundaries of what is possible, unlocking new opportunities and applications that will redefine how we perceive and interact with the visual world.

BOOK 3
PYTHON MACHINE LEARNING AND NEURAL NETWORKS
FROM NOVICE TO PRO

ROB BOTWRIGHT

Chapter 1: Introduction to Machine Learning and Neural Networks

The field of machine learning has undergone a remarkable evolution over the past few decades, transforming from a niche research area into a ubiquitous technology that permeates our daily lives. This evolution has been driven by advances in algorithms, the availability of vast amounts of data, and the exponential growth in computational power.

Machine learning, at its core, is a subfield of artificial intelligence (AI) that focuses on the development of algorithms that enable computers to learn and make predictions or decisions without explicit programming. The idea of machines that can learn from data and improve their performance over time has its roots in the early days of computing.

The concept of machine learning can be traced back to the 1950s and 1960s when pioneers like Arthur Samuel began experimenting with computer programs that could improve their performance in specific tasks through experience. Samuel's work on teaching a computer to play checkers marked one of the earliest instances of machine learning in practice.

However, it wasn't until the late 20th century that machine learning gained significant traction. Advancements in statistical modeling, neural networks, and computational capabilities laid the foundation for modern machine learning.

One of the key turning points in machine learning history came in the 1990s with the resurgence of interest in artificial neural networks, particularly deep neural networks. This resurgence was partly driven by the recognition of the potential of neural networks to model complex patterns in data and the development of more efficient training algorithms.

Deep learning, a subset of machine learning focused on deep neural networks with many layers, has since become a dominant force in the field. The breakthroughs in deep learning have powered many of the recent advancements in image recognition, natural language processing, and reinforcement learning.

The availability of large-scale datasets has played a crucial role in the success of machine learning. With the advent of the internet, massive amounts of data became accessible, enabling researchers and developers to train increasingly complex models. These datasets range from text and images to sensor data, genomics, and more.

The importance of data in machine learning cannot be overstated. Data is the fuel that powers machine learning algorithms, allowing them to learn patterns and make predictions. In essence, machine learning is the process of discovering and encoding patterns present in data.

Machine learning has found applications in diverse domains, revolutionizing industries and solving complex problems. In healthcare, machine learning is used for medical image analysis, drug discovery, and disease prediction. For example, machine learning models can detect anomalies in medical images, aiding radiologists in diagnosing conditions like cancer.

In finance, machine learning algorithms analyze market data to make predictions and optimize trading strategies. Credit scoring models leverage machine learning to assess creditworthiness and reduce risks.

In transportation, machine learning is essential for autonomous vehicles, optimizing route planning, and predicting maintenance needs. Self-driving cars rely on machine learning models to perceive their surroundings and make real-time decisions.

In natural language processing, machine learning enables language translation, sentiment analysis, and chatbots. Voice recognition systems, such as virtual assistants, employ machine learning to understand and respond to spoken language.

E-commerce platforms use machine learning for recommendation systems that suggest products to users based on their preferences and behaviors. These systems have a profound impact on user engagement and sales.

Machine learning has also been instrumental in advancing scientific research. In genomics, machine learning aids in DNA sequence analysis, protein folding prediction, and drug design. Climate scientists use machine learning to analyze vast datasets and make climate predictions.

The adoption of machine learning in these and many other fields has led to significant improvements in accuracy, efficiency, and automation. It has allowed organizations to derive actionable insights from their data and make data-driven decisions.

Machine learning is not without its challenges and limitations. Data privacy concerns, bias in algorithms, and the need for interpretability are some of the ethical and technical issues that researchers and practitioners grapple with. Addressing these challenges is essential to ensure responsible and fair use of machine learning technology.

The democratization of machine learning tools and libraries has made the field accessible to a broader audience. Open-source frameworks like TensorFlow, PyTorch, and scikit-learn have empowered researchers, developers, and businesses to build and deploy machine learning models.

Cloud computing platforms offer scalable infrastructure and machine learning services, making it easier to develop and deploy machine learning solutions. These platforms provide access to powerful hardware, data storage, and pre-built machine learning APIs.

The future of machine learning is full of promise and opportunities. As technology continues to advance, we can expect machine learning models to become even more sophisticated and capable. Areas like reinforcement learning and meta-learning are likely to see significant developments.

Machine learning will continue to shape the future of healthcare, with personalized medicine and disease prediction becoming more precise and accessible. In education, machine learning will play a role in personalized learning experiences and adaptive teaching.

The intersection of machine learning and robotics will lead to advancements in autonomous systems, from self-driving cars to robotic assistants in healthcare and manufacturing. Machine learning models will become more adept at handling multimodal data, incorporating vision, language, and sensor inputs.

Ethical considerations in machine learning will drive the development of fairness, transparency, and accountability mechanisms. Researchers and policymakers will work together to establish guidelines and regulations that promote responsible AI.

Machine learning's impact on society will continue to grow, with applications in fields as diverse as climate science, agriculture, entertainment, and beyond. The evolution of machine learning reflects a journey of innovation, collaboration, and continuous learning.

In summary, the evolution and importance of machine learning have transformed the way we interact with technology and have the potential to revolutionize industries and improve our quality of life. Machine learning has come a long way since its inception, and its future promises to be filled with groundbreaking advancements and transformative applications.

Neural networks serve as the foundation of deep learning, playing a pivotal role in revolutionizing the field of artificial intelligence. These artificial neural networks are inspired by the structure and function of the human brain, consisting of interconnected layers of artificial neurons, or perceptrons.

The concept of neural networks dates back to the 1940s and 1950s when researchers proposed simple models inspired by biological neurons. However, it wasn't until the 1980s that neural networks gained renewed interest and began to exhibit practical success in various applications.

At their core, neural networks are composed of layers, each containing multiple artificial neurons. These layers are typically divided into three categories: input, hidden, and output layers.

In the input layer, the neural network receives data, which can be in the form of numerical values, images, text, or other types of data. Each neuron in the input layer corresponds to a feature or element of the input data.

The hidden layers, as the name suggests, are intermediate layers between the input and output layers. These hidden layers are where the neural network processes and learns patterns from the input data.

Deep learning, a subset of machine learning, focuses on neural networks with multiple hidden layers, often referred to as deep neural networks. These deep networks have the ability to model complex relationships and hierarchical representations in data, making them particularly powerful for tasks like image recognition, natural language processing, and game playing.

The connections between neurons in a neural network are represented by weights, which determine the strength of the connections. During training, these weights are adjusted based on the network's performance on a given task.

The artificial neurons within a neural network apply a mathematical operation to the weighted sum of their inputs. This operation typically involves an activation function, which introduces non-linearity into the network and allows it to learn complex mappings.

Common activation functions include the sigmoid function, hyperbolic tangent (tanh), and rectified linear unit (ReLU). Each of these functions has its own properties and affects the network's ability to model different types of data.

The process of training a neural network involves forward and backward passes. During the forward pass, the input data is passed through the network, and the network's output is compared to the desired or target output.

The difference between the predicted output and the target output, known as the loss or error, is used to compute a gradient during the backward pass. This gradient indicates how the network's weights should be adjusted to minimize the error.

The backpropagation algorithm is a fundamental technique used for adjusting the weights of neural networks based on the gradient of the loss function. This iterative process of forward and backward passes, combined with weight updates, allows the network to learn and improve its performance on the task.

Neural networks are versatile and can be applied to a wide range of tasks, including classification, regression, and generative modeling. Convolutional neural networks (CNNs) excel in image-related tasks by leveraging convolutional layers to extract hierarchical features. Recurrent neural networks (RNNs) are well-suited for sequential data, such as natural language and time series data, thanks to their ability to capture temporal dependencies.

Ensemble methods, which combine the predictions of multiple neural networks, are often used to improve performance and reduce overfitting. Ensemble techniques include bagging, boosting, and stacking, which leverage the diversity of multiple models to make more accurate predictions.

Transfer learning is another important concept in neural networks. It involves using pre-trained neural networks on a related task to bootstrap learning on a new task. This approach has proven highly effective, especially in computer vision and natural language processing.

The availability of pre-trained models, such as Google's Inception, OpenAI's GPT, and Facebook's ResNet, has accelerated progress in various domains. Researchers and practitioners can leverage these models as starting points for their own applications, fine-tuning them on specific tasks.

Neural networks are not without challenges. One common issue is overfitting, where a network performs well on training data but poorly on unseen data. Regularization techniques, data augmentation, and dropout are employed to mitigate overfitting and improve generalization.

Another challenge is the need for large amounts of labeled data. Deep learning models often require extensive datasets for effective training, which can be a limitation in fields where labeled data is scarce or expensive to obtain.

Interpretability is an ongoing challenge in deep learning. As networks become deeper and more complex, understanding their decisions and inner workings can be challenging. Researchers are actively working on methods to make neural networks more interpretable and transparent.

Despite these challenges, neural networks have made significant strides and have had a profound impact on various industries and applications. From autonomous vehicles and healthcare diagnostics to natural language understanding and game playing, deep learning has pushed the boundaries of what is possible in AI.

The future of neural networks is bright, with ongoing research focusing on improving efficiency, reducing the computational cost, and developing more robust and explainable models. As the field continues to evolve, neural networks will continue to be at the forefront of AI innovation, driving advancements that benefit society and reshape the way we interact with technology.

Chapter 2: Python Fundamentals for Machine Learning

Python is a versatile and widely-used programming language known for its simplicity and readability, making it an excellent choice for beginners and experienced developers alike. Understanding the basics of Python and its core data structures is essential for building a strong foundation in programming.

In Python, code blocks are defined by indentation, typically using four spaces or a tab. This indentation-based syntax encourages clean and readable code but requires careful attention to indentation levels.

Python uses dynamic typing, meaning you don't need to declare the data type of a variable explicitly. The interpreter determines the type dynamically at runtime.

Variables in Python are used to store data and can be assigned values of various types, including integers, floating-point numbers, strings, and more. For example, you can assign an integer to a variable like this: **x = 5**.

Python supports both single-line and multi-line comments using the **#** symbol for single-line comments and triple-quotes ("' or """) for multi-line comments.

Data structures are fundamental in Python and provide efficient ways to store, retrieve, and manipulate data. Some of the most commonly used data structures in Python include lists, tuples, sets, and dictionaries.

Lists are ordered collections of items, and you can create a list by enclosing items in square brackets, like this: **my_list = [1, 2, 3]**. You can access list elements using indexing, where the first element has an index of 0.

Tuples are similar to lists but are immutable, meaning their elements cannot be changed after creation. Tuples are defined using parentheses, like this: **my_tuple = (1, 2, 3)**.

Sets are unordered collections of unique items, which means they do not allow duplicate values. You can create a set using curly braces, like this: **my_set = {1, 2, 3}**.

Dictionaries are key-value pairs where each value is associated with a unique key. Dictionaries are defined using curly braces, with key-value pairs separated by colons, like this: **my_dict = {"name": "John", "age": 30}**.

Python provides various operators for performing arithmetic, comparison, and logical operations. These operators include **+**, **-**, __*__, **/**, **==**, **!=**, **>**, **<**, **and**, **or**, and more.

Conditional statements, such as **if**, **elif**, and **else**, allow you to execute different blocks of code based on certain conditions. For example, you can use an **if** statement to check if a condition is true and execute specific code if it is.

Loops are used to repeat a block of code multiple times. Python offers two main types of loops: **for** loops, which iterate over a sequence of items, and **while** loops, which continue as long as a certain condition is true.

Functions are reusable blocks of code that perform a specific task. You can define functions using the **def** keyword, followed by the function name and parameters.

Modularization is a crucial concept in Python, allowing you to organize code into separate modules or files and import them as needed using the **import** statement. This promotes code reuse and maintainability.

Python includes a vast standard library that provides modules for various tasks, such as file I/O, regular expressions, and networking. You can use these modules by importing them into your code.

Exception handling is essential for handling errors and exceptions gracefully. Python provides a **try**, **except**, and **finally** structure to handle exceptions and ensure that your code can recover from unexpected errors.

File I/O operations allow you to read from and write to files on your computer. You can open files using the **open()** function and perform operations like reading, writing, and appending data.

Python supports object-oriented programming (OOP), allowing you to define classes and create objects with attributes and methods. OOP promotes code organization and encapsulation.

Inheritance is a key OOP concept that allows you to create new classes based on existing ones, inheriting their attributes and methods. This facilitates code reuse and hierarchy in class design.

Polymorphism is another OOP concept that enables different objects to respond to the same method or function call in a way that is appropriate for their specific class. This promotes flexibility and extensibility in code design.

Python's built-in data structures, such as lists and dictionaries, can be combined to create more complex data structures. For example, you can create a list of dictionaries to represent a database of records.

List comprehensions are a concise way to create lists based on existing lists, applying a specific operation or filtering criteria. They provide a more readable and Pythonic way to manipulate data.

Generators are a memory-efficient way to create iterators, allowing you to iterate over a sequence of values without loading them all into memory at once. Generators use the **yield** keyword to produce values one at a time.

Decorators are a powerful Python feature that allows you to modify or enhance the behavior of functions or methods without changing their source code. Decorators are often used for tasks like logging, authorization, and performance measurement.

Lambda functions, also known as anonymous functions, allow you to define small, inline functions without explicitly naming them. Lambda functions are often used in situations where a simple function is needed temporarily.

Comprehensions, including list comprehensions, set comprehensions, and dictionary comprehensions, provide concise ways to create and manipulate data structures. These comprehensions enhance code readability and reduce the need for explicit loops.

Python's built-in libraries, such as NumPy for numerical operations and Pandas for data manipulation, extend the language's capabilities for scientific computing and data analysis. These libraries are widely used in fields like data science and machine learning.

Python's simplicity, readability, and extensive ecosystem make it an ideal choice for a wide range of applications, from web development and automation to scientific research and artificial intelligence. Learning the fundamentals of Python and its core data structures is an essential step toward becoming a proficient programmer and unlocking the full potential of this versatile language.

Data manipulation and visualization are essential skills for anyone working with data, whether in the fields of data science, machine learning, or analytics. Python offers powerful libraries and tools that make these tasks efficient and accessible to a wide range of users.

One of the fundamental libraries for data manipulation in Python is Pandas. Pandas provides data structures like DataFrames and Series, which allow you to work with structured data in a flexible and intuitive way.

DataFrames are two-dimensional, tabular data structures that can store and manipulate data with rows and columns. You can think of them as similar to Excel spreadsheets but with powerful programming capabilities.

Series, on the other hand, are one-dimensional data structures that are useful for storing and analyzing sequences of data. They can be thought of as a single column of a DataFrame.

Pandas allows you to read data from various file formats, such as CSV, Excel, and SQL databases, making it easy to import and analyze data from different sources. You can use commands like **pd.read_csv()** or **pd.read_excel()** to load data into Pandas DataFrames.

Once you have your data in a DataFrame, Pandas provides a wide range of functions for data cleaning, transformation, and exploration. You can perform tasks like filtering rows, selecting columns, and aggregating data using intuitive and expressive syntax.

For example, you can use the **.head()** method to quickly inspect the first few rows of a DataFrame and get an overview of its contents. Similarly, the **.describe()** method provides summary statistics for numerical columns, helping you understand the data distribution.

Data cleaning is a crucial step in data analysis, and Pandas offers methods to handle missing values, duplicate rows, and outliers. You can use commands like **.dropna()**, **.fillna()**, and **.duplicated()** to clean your data effectively.

Pandas also supports powerful data transformation operations, such as merging, joining, and pivoting. These operations are essential when working with multiple datasets or when you need to reshape your data for analysis or visualization.

When it comes to data visualization, Python offers a range of libraries, with Matplotlib being one of the most widely used.

Matplotlib provides a versatile platform for creating static, animated, or interactive plots and charts.

You can use Matplotlib to create various types of plots, including line plots, scatter plots, bar plots, histograms, and more. With a few lines of code, you can customize the appearance and style of your plots to suit your needs.

Matplotlib's integration with Jupyter notebooks makes it a popular choice for data exploration and analysis. You can easily visualize data within the notebook environment and share your findings with others.

Another powerful library for data visualization is Seaborn, built on top of Matplotlib. Seaborn simplifies the creation of attractive statistical plots and offers additional features like automatic color palettes and style themes.

Seaborn's functions are designed to work seamlessly with Pandas DataFrames, making it easy to visualize patterns and relationships in your data. You can create complex plots like heatmaps, pair plots, and violin plots with just a few lines of code.

For interactive data visualization, libraries like Plotly and Bokeh are popular choices. These libraries allow you to create interactive plots that can be embedded in web applications or shared online.

Plotly provides a high-level interface for creating interactive charts, maps, and dashboards. You can add features like hover tooltips, zooming, and panning to your visualizations with ease.

Bokeh, on the other hand, is a versatile library for building interactive, web-based data applications. It offers powerful tools for creating interactive plots and widgets, making it suitable for creating data-driven web applications.

When working with geographical data, libraries like Folium and Basemap are valuable for creating maps and visualizing spatial information. Folium is particularly well-suited for creating interactive maps that can be embedded in web applications.

Python's data manipulation and visualization capabilities extend beyond Pandas and Matplotlib. In the field of data science, libraries like Scikit-learn provide tools for machine learning, including data preprocessing, model training, and evaluation.

Scikit-learn offers a wide range of machine learning algorithms and models, making it a go-to choice for tasks like classification, regression, clustering, and dimensionality reduction. The library's consistent API and extensive documentation make it accessible to both beginners and experienced data scientists.

For more advanced machine learning tasks, libraries like TensorFlow and PyTorch are popular choices. These deep learning frameworks enable you to build and train neural networks for tasks like image recognition, natural language processing, and reinforcement learning.

Python's ecosystem also includes specialized libraries for time series analysis, such as Statsmodels and Prophet, which are widely used in finance and forecasting.

In addition to data manipulation and visualization libraries, Python offers numerous packages for statistical analysis and hypothesis testing. Statsmodels, for instance, provides tools for estimating and interpreting statistical models, including linear regression, time series analysis, and generalized linear models.

Jupyter notebooks are a valuable tool for combining code, text, and visualizations in a single interactive document. They are widely used in data analysis and data science projects to document and share findings.

Chapter 3: Data Preprocessing and Feature Engineering

Data cleaning and transformation are critical steps in the data preparation process, ensuring that your data is accurate, consistent, and suitable for analysis or modeling.

Cleaning involves identifying and correcting errors or inconsistencies in your dataset, such as missing values, duplicate records, or outliers.

One common data cleaning task is handling missing values, which can arise due to various reasons, including data collection errors or incomplete records.

Python provides tools like Pandas to efficiently handle missing data, allowing you to drop or fill missing values based on your analysis requirements.

Another aspect of data cleaning is dealing with duplicate records, which can distort your analysis results or model performance.

Pandas offers methods like **.duplicated()** to identify duplicates and **.drop_duplicates()** to remove them, helping you maintain data integrity.

Outliers, extreme values that deviate significantly from the majority of your data, can also impact analysis or modeling outcomes.

You can use statistical techniques or visualization tools to identify and address outliers, ensuring they don't unduly influence your results.

Inconsistent data formats, such as dates in different styles or units in various systems, can pose challenges during analysis.

Transforming data to a consistent format is essential for accurate analysis, and Pandas provides functions for such conversions.

Standardizing or normalizing numeric variables to a common scale is crucial for some machine learning algorithms, preventing features with larger scales from dominating the model.

Python libraries like Scikit-learn offer preprocessing tools for scaling and transforming data as needed.

Handling categorical variables, which represent categories or labels rather than numerical values, is another aspect of data transformation.

One-hot encoding, label encoding, or custom transformations can convert categorical variables into a format suitable for analysis or modeling.

Data cleaning and transformation also involve creating new features or variables based on existing data, a process known as feature engineering.

Feature engineering aims to extract meaningful information or relationships from your data, improving model performance or analysis insights.

Python libraries like Pandas, NumPy, and Scikit-learn offer versatile tools for feature engineering tasks, such as creating interaction terms, aggregating data, or extracting text features.

In addition to cleaning and transforming data, it's essential to validate the quality and integrity of your dataset.

Data validation involves checking for inconsistencies, outliers, or errors that might have been missed during the cleaning process.

Visualizations and statistical summaries are valuable for assessing data quality and identifying potential issues.

Exploratory data analysis (EDA) is a crucial step in understanding your dataset's characteristics and relationships between variables.

Python libraries like Matplotlib, Seaborn, and Plotly provide powerful visualization capabilities to support EDA.

During EDA, you can generate various plots and charts, including histograms, scatter plots, box plots, and correlation matrices, to uncover patterns and insights.

Descriptive statistics, such as measures of central tendency, dispersion, and distribution, complement visualizations and help summarize your data's key properties.

Effective data cleaning and transformation require a clear understanding of the domain and the specific goals of your analysis or modeling project.

Collaboration with domain experts can help ensure that your data preparation steps align with the real-world context of your data.

Data pipelines or workflows, built using Python libraries like Apache Airflow or Luigi, can automate data cleaning and transformation processes, streamlining repetitive tasks and ensuring consistency.

Data cleaning and transformation are iterative processes, requiring constant refinement as new insights are gained and models are developed.

Reproducibility and documentation of data cleaning and transformation steps are crucial for maintaining transparency and replicability in your analysis or modeling projects.

Data cleaning and transformation are not isolated tasks but integral components of the broader data science or analytics lifecycle, influencing the quality and reliability of your results.

By investing time and effort in these critical steps, you can unlock the full potential of your data and improve the accuracy and validity of your analysis or modeling outcomes.

In summary, data cleaning and transformation are essential for preparing data for analysis or modeling in Python. These processes involve handling missing values, duplicates, outliers, and inconsistent formats, as well as encoding categorical variables and performing feature engineering. Python libraries like Pandas, Scikit-learn, and visualization tools such as Matplotlib and Seaborn provide the necessary functionalities to perform these tasks effectively. Data validation, exploratory data analysis, and collaboration with domain experts are also essential aspects of data preparation. By prioritizing data quality and transparency, you can enhance the reliability and impact of your data-driven projects.

Feature extraction and selection techniques are fundamental in data analysis and machine learning, playing a critical role in improving model performance and interpretability.

Feature extraction involves transforming raw data into a reduced representation that retains relevant information while reducing dimensionality.

Principal Component Analysis (PCA) is a popular technique for feature extraction that identifies orthogonal components capturing the most significant variance in the data.

Python's Scikit-learn library provides a simple interface for performing PCA using the **PCA** class.

Another technique for feature extraction is Linear Discriminant Analysis (LDA), which focuses on maximizing class separability in classification problems.

LDA is particularly useful when you have labeled data, and Scikit-learn offers an **LDA** class for implementing it.

Feature extraction can also be achieved through domain-specific methods, such as text vectorization techniques like TF-IDF or word embeddings for natural language processing tasks.

Selecting the most relevant features from a dataset is crucial for improving model efficiency and preventing overfitting.

Filter methods involve ranking features based on statistical measures like correlation, mutual information, or chi-squared tests.

Python's Scikit-learn provides functions for feature selection, including **SelectKBest** and **SelectPercentile** for filter-based selection.

Wrapper methods assess feature subsets' performance using a specific machine learning algorithm, making them computationally expensive but effective.

The Recursive Feature Elimination (RFE) algorithm is an example of a wrapper method, available in Scikit-learn's **RFE** class.

Embedded methods combine feature selection with the model training process, allowing algorithms to automatically choose the most relevant features.

Lasso and Ridge regression are examples of embedded methods that perform feature selection while regularizing the model.

Machine learning libraries like XGBoost, LightGBM, and Scikit-learn offer built-in feature selection capabilities through techniques like importance scores or recursive feature elimination.

Regularization techniques like L1 regularization in logistic regression or linear support vector machines also perform implicit feature selection by shrinking coefficients to zero.

Exploratory Data Analysis (EDA) plays a crucial role in understanding feature importance and relationships within your data.

Python's libraries for data visualization, such as Matplotlib, Seaborn, and Plotly, provide powerful tools for visualizing feature distributions, correlations, and patterns.

Feature importance can be assessed using tree-based models like Random Forest or Gradient Boosting, which assign scores to features based on their contribution to model predictions.

Python's Scikit-learn library offers built-in functions for calculating feature importances from these models.

Recursive Feature Elimination (RFE) is a wrapper-based method that recursively removes the least important features, ranking them by their impact on model performance.

The Recursive Feature Elimination with Cross-Validation (RFECV) variant, available in Scikit-learn, selects features while considering cross-validation to prevent overfitting.

Feature selection can also be guided by domain knowledge, where subject matter experts identify and prioritize relevant features based on their expertise.

Hybrid approaches combine multiple feature selection techniques to leverage their strengths while mitigating weaknesses.

For example, you can use a filter method to preselect features based on statistical tests and then apply a wrapper method to further refine the selection.

The choice of feature extraction and selection techniques depends on your specific problem, dataset, and machine learning algorithm.

It's essential to experiment with different methods and evaluate their impact on model performance using techniques like cross-validation.

Python's Scikit-learn library provides a unified interface for various feature extraction and selection methods, making it convenient for experimentation and integration into machine learning pipelines.

Automated feature selection tools, such as Boruta and Featuretools, offer efficient ways to identify and select relevant features without extensive manual intervention.

Feature engineering, the process of creating new features from existing ones, complements feature extraction and selection.

Feature engineering can involve mathematical transformations, interaction terms, or aggregations that capture meaningful relationships in the data.

Python's Pandas library is a powerful tool for feature engineering, allowing you to create and manipulate features efficiently.

Feature extraction and selection are not one-time tasks but ongoing processes that should be revisited as new data becomes available or as your problem domain evolves.

It's important to monitor feature relevance and model performance over time to ensure that your selected features remain effective.

Interpretable machine learning models, like linear regression or decision trees, can provide insights into feature importance and relationships, aiding in feature selection decisions.

Explainable AI (XAI) techniques, such as SHAP (SHapley Additive exPlanations) values, provide model-agnostic explanations for individual feature contributions to predictions.

Feature extraction and selection are essential for model efficiency, interpretability, and generalization.

By reducing dimensionality and focusing on the most relevant features, you can build more efficient models that are easier to understand and maintain.

In summary, feature extraction and selection are crucial steps in the data preprocessing and machine learning pipeline.

Python's rich ecosystem of libraries, including Scikit-learn, Pandas, and various visualization tools, provides comprehensive support for these tasks.

Choosing the right feature extraction and selection methods depends on your problem, dataset, and modeling goals. Regularly revisiting and refining your feature selection process can lead to more robust and interpretable machine learning models.

Chapter 4: Supervised Learning Algorithms and Models

Regression models are a class of statistical models used for predicting a continuous target variable based on one or more input features.

They play a vital role in various fields, including economics, finance, biology, and machine learning.

The fundamental idea behind regression is to find a mathematical relationship between the input features and the target variable that can be used for making predictions.

One of the simplest forms of regression is linear regression, where the relationship between the input features and the target variable is assumed to be linear.

In linear regression, the goal is to find the best-fitting line (or hyperplane in higher dimensions) that minimizes the sum of squared differences between the predicted values and the actual target values.

Python offers several libraries for implementing linear regression, including Scikit-learn, Statsmodels, and TensorFlow.

Scikit-learn is a popular choice for beginners due to its ease of use and extensive documentation.

To perform linear regression with Scikit-learn, you can use the **LinearRegression** class, which provides methods for fitting the model to your data, making predictions, and evaluating its performance.

Another variant of linear regression is multiple linear regression, where there are multiple input features instead of just one.

This allows you to model the relationship between the target variable and multiple predictors, which can be more realistic in many real-world scenarios.

Polynomial regression is another extension of linear regression, where the relationship between the target variable and the input features is assumed to be polynomial. This allows you to capture more complex relationships between variables, such as curves or waves.

Python's libraries provide tools for implementing polynomial regression, including Scikit-learn's **PolynomialFeatures** class, which allows you to create polynomial features from your input data.

Regularization techniques like Lasso and Ridge regression are used to prevent overfitting in linear regression models.

Lasso adds a penalty term to the linear regression equation that encourages some coefficients to become exactly zero, effectively performing feature selection.

Ridge regression adds a penalty term that discourages large coefficients, making the model more robust to multicollinearity.

In Scikit-learn, you can use the **Lasso** and **Ridge** classes to implement these regularization techniques.

Evaluating the performance of a regression model is crucial to ensure that it makes accurate predictions.

Common metrics for regression evaluation include Mean Squared Error (MSE), Root Mean Squared Error (RMSE), Mean Absolute Error (MAE), and R-squared (R^2).

MSE measures the average squared difference between predicted and actual values, RMSE is the square root of MSE, and MAE measures the average absolute difference.

R-squared, on the other hand, quantifies how well the model explains the variance in the target variable, with higher values indicating a better fit.

Python libraries like Scikit-learn provide functions for calculating these metrics, making it easy to assess your model's performance.

Cross-validation is a crucial technique for estimating a model's performance on unseen data and preventing overfitting.

K-fold cross-validation involves splitting the data into K subsets, training the model on K-1 subsets, and evaluating it on the remaining subset.

This process is repeated K times, with each subset serving as the validation set once.

Python's Scikit-learn library provides functions for performing cross-validation with regression models.

Another powerful regression technique is decision tree regression, which models the relationship between input features and the target variable as a tree structure.

Each internal node of the tree represents a decision based on one of the input features, and each leaf node contains a prediction.

Decision tree regression is capable of capturing complex non-linear relationships in the data, making it a valuable tool for various regression problems.

Python's Scikit-learn library offers a **DecisionTreeRegressor** class for implementing decision tree regression.

Random Forest regression is an ensemble method that combines multiple decision trees to improve predictive accuracy and reduce overfitting.

It works by training multiple decision tree regressors on random subsets of the data and averaging their predictions.

Python's Scikit-learn library provides a **RandomForestRegressor** class for implementing random forest regression.

Gradient Boosting regression is another ensemble method that builds an additive model by training decision trees sequentially.

Each tree corrects the errors made by the previous ones, gradually improving prediction accuracy.

Scikit-learn offers a **GradientBoostingRegressor** class for implementing gradient boosting regression.

Support Vector Machine (SVM) regression is a powerful technique for modeling non-linear relationships between input features and the target variable.

It works by mapping the input features to a higher-dimensional space and finding a hyperplane that best fits the data.

Python's Scikit-learn library provides an **SVR** class for implementing SVM regression.

Neural networks, specifically feedforward neural networks, can also be used for regression tasks.

They consist of multiple layers of interconnected neurons and are capable of learning complex non-linear relationships in the data.

Python's deep learning frameworks, such as TensorFlow and PyTorch, provide tools for building and training neural network regression models.

Time series regression is a specialized form of regression used for forecasting future values based on historical time-ordered data.

It takes into account the temporal nature of the data and can capture seasonality, trends, and other patterns.

Python's libraries like Statsmodels and Prophet offer tools for time series regression.

AutoML (Automated Machine Learning) tools like Auto-sklearn and TPOT can automate the process of selecting the best regression model and hyperparameters, saving time and effort.

In summary, regression models are essential tools for predicting continuous target variables based on input features.

Python provides a rich ecosystem of libraries and frameworks for implementing various regression techniques, from simple linear regression to complex neural networks.

Evaluating model performance, selecting appropriate features, and applying regularization techniques are crucial steps in building effective regression models.

Whether you're working on financial forecasting, sales prediction, or any other regression problem, Python's versatile tools and libraries can help you build accurate and reliable models.

Classification algorithms are a fundamental part of machine learning, focusing on categorizing data into predefined classes or labels based on input features.

These algorithms are essential for various applications, such as spam email detection, sentiment analysis, medical diagnosis, and image recognition.

The goal of classification is to learn a mapping from input features to discrete output labels, enabling automated decision-making.

One of the simplest and most commonly used classification algorithms is logistic regression, which models the probability of an input belonging to a particular class.

In logistic regression, a sigmoid function is used to transform the linear combination of input features into a probability score between 0 and 1.

Python's Scikit-learn library provides an easy-to-use implementation of logistic regression for binary and multiclass classification problems.

Decision trees are another powerful classification algorithm that models decisions as a tree structure.

Each internal node represents a decision based on a feature, and each leaf node corresponds to a class label.

Decision trees are interpretable and can capture complex decision boundaries, making them valuable for various applications.

Scikit-learn offers a **DecisionTreeClassifier** class for implementing decision tree-based classification.

Random Forest is an ensemble method that combines multiple decision trees to improve classification accuracy and reduce overfitting.

It works by training a collection of decision trees on random subsets of the data and averaging their predictions.

Python's Scikit-learn library provides a **RandomForestClassifier** class for random forest-based classification.

Gradient Boosting is another ensemble method used for classification, sequentially training decision trees to correct the errors of the previous ones.

It builds an additive model that gradually improves prediction accuracy.

Scikit-learn offers a **GradientBoostingClassifier** class for implementing gradient boosting-based classification.

Support Vector Machines (SVM) are classification algorithms that find a hyperplane to separate data points into different classes.

SVM aims to maximize the margin between data points of different classes, making it effective for both linear and non-linear classification tasks.

Python's Scikit-learn library provides an **SVC** class for implementing support vector machine-based classification.

k-Nearest Neighbors (k-NN) is a simple yet effective classification algorithm that assigns labels to data points based on the majority class among their k-nearest neighbors. The choice of the value k influences the algorithm's sensitivity to noise and model complexity.

Scikit-learn includes a **KNeighborsClassifier** class for k-NN classification.

Naive Bayes classification is based on Bayes' theorem and assumes that input features are conditionally independent given the class label.

Despite its simplifying assumption, Naive Bayes can perform well in various classification tasks, such as text classification.

Scikit-learn offers several Naive Bayes classifiers, including **MultinomialNB** and **GaussianNB**.

Neural networks, specifically feedforward neural networks, are versatile tools for classification tasks.

They consist of interconnected layers of neurons and can model complex non-linear relationships in the data.

Deep learning frameworks like TensorFlow and PyTorch provide tools for building and training neural network-based classifiers.

Logistic regression, despite its simplicity, is a powerful algorithm for binary classification tasks.

It is widely used in applications such as medical diagnosis, spam detection, and credit scoring.

Python's Scikit-learn library allows you to perform binary classification using logistic regression with ease.

For multiclass classification, logistic regression can be extended to a one-vs-all or softmax approach.

In one-vs-all, you train a binary logistic regression classifier for each class, treating it as the positive class and all others as the negative class.

The final prediction is based on the classifier with the highest probability score.

In the softmax approach, you use the softmax function to compute the probabilities of each class, and the class with the highest probability is selected as the prediction.

Random Forest is a versatile ensemble algorithm that can handle both binary and multiclass classification problems effectively.

It combines multiple decision trees to improve predictive accuracy and reduce overfitting.

Random Forest is resistant to overfitting, making it a reliable choice for many classification tasks.

Gradient Boosting is another ensemble technique that excels in both binary and multiclass classification.

It builds an additive model of decision trees, sequentially correcting the errors made by the previous trees.

Gradient Boosting is particularly suitable for complex and high-dimensional data.

Support Vector Machines (SVM) can be used for both binary and multiclass classification by extending the basic formulation.

For multiclass SVM, you can use the one-vs-one or one-vs-all approach.

In the one-vs-one approach, you train a binary SVM classifier for every pair of classes, and the class with the most votes is the final prediction.

In the one-vs-all approach, each class is treated as the positive class, and all others are considered the negative class.

k-Nearest Neighbors (k-NN) is a simple yet effective algorithm for both binary and multiclass classification.

It assigns a data point to the class that is most frequent among its k-nearest neighbors.

The choice of the value k influences the model's sensitivity to noise and its generalization performance.

Naive Bayes classifiers are probabilistic models that work well for both binary and multiclass classification tasks.

They are based on Bayes' theorem and assume that input features are conditionally independent given the class label.

Naive Bayes classifiers are particularly suitable for text classification, spam detection, and sentiment analysis.

Neural networks, specifically feedforward neural networks, are powerful tools for binary and multiclass classification.

They consist of multiple layers of interconnected neurons and can model complex non-linear relationships in the data.

Deep learning frameworks like TensorFlow and PyTorch provide comprehensive support for building and training neural network classifiers.

Evaluating the performance of a classification model is crucial to assess its accuracy and reliability.

Common metrics for binary classification include accuracy, precision, recall, F1-score, and ROC-AUC.

Accuracy measures the percentage of correctly classified instances, while precision quantifies the proportion of true positive predictions among all positive predictions.

Recall measures the proportion of true positive predictions among all actual positive instances.

F1-score is the harmonic mean of precision and recall, providing a balance between the two.

ROC-AUC (Receiver Operating Characteristic - Area Under the Curve) is a metric that assesses the model's ability to discriminate between positive and negative classes.

For multiclass classification, you can use metrics like accuracy, precision, recall, F1-score, and confusion matrices.

Confusion matrices provide a detailed breakdown of the model's predictions, showing true positives, true negatives, false positives, and false negatives for each class.

Cross-validation is a crucial technique for estimating a classification model's performance on unseen data and preventing overfitting.

K-fold cross-validation involves dividing the data into K subsets, training the model on K-1 subsets, and evaluating it on the remaining subset.

This process is repeated K times, with each subset serving as the validation set once.

Hyperparameter tuning is essential to optimize the performance of a classification model.

Hyperparameters are parameters that are not learned from the data but affect the model's behavior.

Grid search and random search are common methods for hyperparameter tuning, where different combinations of hyperparameters are evaluated to find the best configuration.

In summary, classification algorithms are essential tools for automating decision-making tasks based on input features.

Python's Scikit-learn library provides a wide range of implementations for various classification algorithms, making it accessible and convenient for both beginners and experts.

Evaluating model performance, selecting appropriate metrics, and tuning hyperparameters are crucial steps in building effective classification models for binary and multiclass tasks.

Whether you're working on sentiment analysis, image recognition, or any other classification problem, Python's rich ecosystem of tools and libraries can help you build accurate and reliable classifiers.

Chapter 5: Unsupervised Learning and Clustering Techniques

Clustering methods are a class of unsupervised machine learning techniques used to discover patterns or group similar data points together.

These methods play a crucial role in various fields, including data analysis, image processing, customer segmentation, and anomaly detection.

The fundamental idea behind clustering is to group data points that are more similar to each other than to those in other groups.

One of the most well-known clustering algorithms is K-means, which partitions data into K clusters by minimizing the sum of squared distances between data points and the centroid of their respective clusters.

K-means is widely used due to its simplicity and efficiency, making it suitable for large datasets.

Python's Scikit-learn library provides an easy-to-use implementation of the K-means algorithm.

Hierarchical clustering is another popular method that organizes data points into a hierarchical tree-like structure called a dendrogram.

This tree structure represents the relationships between data points and can be used to create clusters at different levels of granularity.

Agglomerative and divisive are the two main approaches to hierarchical clustering, where the former starts with individual data points as clusters and merges them, while the latter begins with one cluster and splits it.

DBSCAN (Density-Based Spatial Clustering of Applications with Noise) is a density-based clustering algorithm that groups data points based on their density and connectivity.

DBSCAN is capable of discovering clusters of arbitrary shapes and can identify outliers as noise.

It is particularly useful for datasets with non-uniform cluster densities.

Python's Scikit-learn library offers an implementation of DBSCAN.

Gaussian Mixture Models (GMMs) are probabilistic models that represent data points as a mixture of multiple Gaussian distributions.

GMMs model the underlying data distribution as a combination of these Gaussian components, each representing a cluster.

Expectation-Maximization (EM) is the main algorithm used for fitting GMMs to data.

Scikit-learn provides a **GaussianMixture** class for GMM-based clustering.

Agglomerative clustering is a hierarchical method that starts with individual data points as clusters and iteratively merges the closest clusters until a single cluster remains.

This process can be visualized using a dendrogram, which allows you to choose the number of clusters based on your specific needs.

Divisive clustering, on the other hand, begins with a single cluster that contains all data points and recursively splits it into smaller clusters.

Agglomerative and divisive clustering methods are complementary, offering different perspectives on the data's hierarchical structure.

Density-based clustering methods, like DBSCAN, are capable of finding clusters of arbitrary shapes and can identify noisy data points as outliers.

These methods rely on the concept of data point density and connectivity to group similar points together.

Gaussian Mixture Models (GMMs) are probabilistic models that describe the data as a mixture of multiple Gaussian distributions.

Each Gaussian component represents a cluster, and GMMs can capture complex patterns in the data, even when clusters have different shapes and sizes.

Spectral clustering is a graph-based approach that treats data points as nodes in a graph and clusters them based on the graph's eigenvectors.

Spectral clustering can uncover non-linear relationships between data points and is useful for image segmentation and community detection in networks.

Clustering algorithms can be categorized into two main types: partitional and hierarchical.

Partitional methods, like K-means and GMMs, divide the data into non-overlapping clusters, while hierarchical methods create a nested structure of clusters.

The choice between partitional and hierarchical clustering depends on the nature of the data and the desired level of granularity in the clusters.

Clustering is an unsupervised learning task, meaning that it doesn't require labeled data for training.

Instead, it relies on the inherent patterns and similarities within the data to create meaningful clusters.

Evaluating the quality of clustering results can be challenging because it often depends on the specific problem and the domain knowledge of the data.

Some common metrics used for clustering evaluation include silhouette score, Davies-Bouldin index, and the Dunn index.

Silhouette score measures the similarity of data points within the same cluster compared to other clusters, with values ranging from -1 to 1, where higher values indicate better clustering.

Davies-Bouldin index assesses the average similarity between each cluster and its most similar cluster, with lower values indicating better clustering.

The Dunn index measures the ratio of the minimum inter-cluster distance to the maximum intra-cluster distance, with higher values indicating better clustering.

Selecting the appropriate clustering algorithm and the number of clusters (K) can be challenging and may require experimentation.

Techniques like the elbow method, silhouette analysis, and the Davies-Bouldin index can help determine the optimal number of clusters.

The elbow method involves plotting the variance explained as a function of the number of clusters and looking for an "elbow" point where the explained variance starts to level off.

Silhouette analysis calculates the silhouette score for different values of K and helps identify the number of clusters that maximizes the score.

The Davies-Bouldin index quantifies the average similarity between each cluster and its most similar neighbor, helping select K with the lowest index value.

In summary, clustering methods are essential tools for discovering patterns and grouping similar data points together.

Different clustering algorithms offer various advantages and are suitable for different types of data and problem domains.

Evaluating the quality of clustering results is essential and can be challenging, often requiring the use of multiple metrics and visualization techniques.

Selecting the right clustering algorithm and determining the optimal number of clusters depend on the specific problem and may require experimentation and domain knowledge.

Dimensionality reduction techniques are essential tools in the field of machine learning and data analysis, helping to simplify complex datasets and improve the efficiency and effectiveness of various algorithms.
These techniques are particularly valuable when dealing with high-dimensional data, where the number of features or variables is significantly larger than the number of data points.
High-dimensional data often poses challenges in terms of computational complexity, visualization, and the risk of overfitting.
One common dimensionality reduction method is Principal Component Analysis (PCA), which aims to find a lower-dimensional representation of the data while retaining as much of the original variance as possible.
PCA identifies a set of orthogonal axes, known as principal components, along which the data exhibits the most variation.
The first principal component captures the most variance, the second captures the second most, and so on.
By choosing a subset of these principal components, you can reduce the dimensionality of the data while preserving the essential information.
Another dimensionality reduction technique is t-Distributed Stochastic Neighbor Embedding (t-SNE), which focuses on visualizing high-dimensional data in a lower-dimensional space, typically two or three dimensions.
t-SNE emphasizes the preservation of pairwise similarities between data points, making it suitable for data visualization and clustering.

However, t-SNE is not suitable for dimensionality reduction for computational purposes.

Linear Discriminant Analysis (LDA) is a dimensionality reduction technique that aims to maximize the separability between different classes or categories in the data.

LDA seeks a lower-dimensional space where the classes are well-separated, making it useful for tasks like classification and feature extraction.

LDA can be considered both a classification and dimensionality reduction method.

Autoencoders are a class of neural networks used for unsupervised learning and dimensionality reduction.

They consist of an encoder network that maps high-dimensional data to a lower-dimensional representation and a decoder network that reconstructs the original data from the reduced representation.

Autoencoders learn to capture the essential features of the data in the lower-dimensional space, making them useful for tasks like image denoising, anomaly detection, and feature learning.

Kernel PCA is an extension of PCA that leverages kernel functions to perform nonlinear dimensionality reduction.

Kernel PCA projects the data into a higher-dimensional space where linear PCA can effectively reduce dimensionality.

This technique is particularly useful when the underlying data distribution is non-linear.

t-SNE, as previously mentioned, is a powerful method for visualizing high-dimensional data in a lower-dimensional space.

It uses a probability distribution to model pairwise similarities between data points in the high-dimensional space and the lower-dimensional space.

By minimizing the divergence between these two probability distributions, t-SNE maps data points to a lower-dimensional representation while preserving their relative similarities.

Non-Negative Matrix Factorization (NMF) is a dimensionality reduction technique that factorizes a non-negative data matrix into two lower-dimensional matrices.

NMF is commonly used for feature extraction, topic modeling, and image processing.

It enforces non-negativity constraints, which can be beneficial when dealing with non-negative data, such as images or text.

Random Projection is a dimensionality reduction technique that uses random matrices to project high-dimensional data onto a lower-dimensional subspace.

Random Projection can provide significant dimensionality reduction benefits with reduced computational cost compared to some other methods.

It is particularly useful when computational efficiency is a primary concern.

Sparse Coding is a dimensionality reduction technique that seeks a sparse representation of data, where only a small number of coefficients are non-zero.

Sparse Coding is used in various applications, including image processing, natural language processing, and feature learning.

It can effectively reduce dimensionality while preserving important features.

When selecting a dimensionality reduction technique, it's essential to consider the specific problem at hand and the characteristics of the data.

PCA is a versatile and widely used method for linear dimensionality reduction and visualization.

LDA is valuable when the goal is to maximize class separability, making it useful for classification tasks.

t-SNE is excellent for visualizing high-dimensional data, but it doesn't provide a lower-dimensional representation for computational purposes.

Autoencoders are powerful for unsupervised feature learning and data reconstruction tasks.

Kernel PCA and NMF are useful when dealing with non-linear data distributions, while Random Projection offers efficiency benefits.

Sparse Coding is valuable for sparse representations and feature selection.

The choice of dimensionality reduction technique should align with the specific goals of the analysis and the nature of the data.

Moreover, it's essential to assess the impact of dimensionality reduction on downstream tasks, such as classification or clustering, to ensure that the reduced representation retains the necessary information for the desired outcomes.

In summary, dimensionality reduction techniques are essential tools in the field of machine learning and data analysis.

They help simplify complex datasets, improve computational efficiency, and enable effective visualization.

The choice of technique should be guided by the specific goals of the analysis and the nature of the data, considering factors such as linearity, class separability, and computational efficiency.

Dimensionality reduction plays a crucial role in preprocessing and feature engineering, contributing to the success of various machine learning tasks.

Chapter 6: Neural Networks and Deep Learning Basics

Activation functions and loss functions are fundamental components of neural networks, playing critical roles in shaping the behavior and training process of these complex models.

Activation functions serve as the mathematical operations applied to neuron outputs, introducing non-linearity into the network and enabling it to model complex relationships in data.

Common activation functions include the sigmoid function, which squashes input values into a range between 0 and 1, making it suitable for binary classification tasks where the output represents probabilities.

The hyperbolic tangent (tanh) function is similar to the sigmoid but squashes inputs between -1 and 1, making it zero-centered and sometimes more effective for training deep networks.

The rectified linear unit (ReLU) is a widely used activation function that outputs the input if it is positive and zero otherwise, which introduces sparsity and helps mitigate the vanishing gradient problem.

Leaky ReLU and Parametric ReLU (PReLU) variants address the issue of dying ReLU units by allowing a small, non-zero gradient for negative inputs.

Exponential Linear Unit (ELU) is another activation function that smooths out the negative side of the ReLU, offering improved performance and robustness.

Activation functions like Swish and GELU have also gained popularity, particularly in deep learning models, for their empirical advantages in training.

Choosing the right activation function depends on the specific task and the behavior you want the neurons to exhibit in your network.

For instance, ReLU variants are often preferred in deep convolutional neural networks (CNNs) for image processing tasks, while tanh or sigmoid may be suitable for certain recurrent neural networks (RNNs) used in sequence modeling.

Loss functions, on the other hand, are used to measure the discrepancy between the network's predictions and the actual target values during training.

The choice of a loss function depends on the type of problem the neural network aims to solve.

For regression tasks, where the goal is to predict continuous values, the Mean Squared Error (MSE) loss is a common choice.

MSE calculates the average squared difference between predictions and targets, providing a measure of how well the model's outputs match the actual values.

For binary classification tasks, where the goal is to distinguish between two classes, the Binary Cross-Entropy loss (or Log Loss) is frequently used.

Binary Cross-Entropy measures the dissimilarity between predicted probabilities and actual binary labels, encouraging the model to assign higher probabilities to the correct class.

For multi-class classification tasks, where there are more than two classes, the Categorical Cross-Entropy loss is a suitable choice.

Categorical Cross-Entropy quantifies the difference between predicted class probabilities and one-hot encoded target vectors, encouraging the model to assign high probabilities to the correct class while penalizing errors for other classes.

Hinge loss is often used in support vector machines (SVMs) and some deep learning models for classification tasks.

It encourages a margin of separation between classes, making it suitable for binary and multi-class classification problems.

Other loss functions, such as Huber loss and quantile loss, are employed for specific regression tasks or when robustness to outliers is needed.

The choice of a loss function is critical because it guides the learning process of the neural network.

Different loss functions introduce different gradients during backpropagation, affecting how the model updates its weights and biases.

Optimizing the correct loss function aligns the model's training objectives with the task requirements, ultimately leading to better performance.

In some cases, custom loss functions may be designed to address specific objectives or constraints unique to a particular problem.

For example, in object detection tasks, a custom loss function might consider both localization accuracy and classification accuracy, reflecting the dual nature of the problem.

Furthermore, loss functions can be augmented with regularization terms to prevent overfitting.

L1 and L2 regularization, also known as Lasso and Ridge regularization, respectively, add penalties to the loss based on the magnitudes of the model's weights.

These penalties encourage weight values to remain small, reducing the risk of overfitting by preventing individual weights from becoming too large.

Elastic Net regularization combines L1 and L2 regularization, offering a balance between sparsity and weight decay.

In summary, activation functions and loss functions are fundamental components of neural networks, with activation functions introducing non-linearity into neurons and loss functions measuring the model's performance during training.

The choice of activation function depends on the desired behavior of the neurons, while the selection of a loss function depends on the type of task the neural network is designed for.

Custom loss functions and regularization techniques can be employed to address specific problem requirements and mitigate overfitting.

These components collectively shape the architecture and training process of neural networks, playing a pivotal role in their effectiveness across various domains and applications.

Setting up the deep learning environment is a crucial step in embarking on your journey into the world of artificial intelligence and machine learning.

Before diving into the exciting world of deep learning, you'll need to ensure that your computing environment is properly configured to support the development and training of neural networks.

To get started, you'll need a computer with sufficient computational power, which can range from a standard laptop to a high-performance workstation or cloud-based virtual machine.

For most beginners, a laptop with a dedicated graphics processing unit (GPU) or access to cloud-based GPU resources is often sufficient for learning and experimentation.

Once you have your hardware in place, the next step is to choose the right operating system for your deep learning tasks.

Common choices include Windows, macOS, and various Linux distributions, with Ubuntu being a popular choice among researchers and developers due to its compatibility with many deep learning libraries and frameworks.

Installing a package manager, such as Anaconda or Miniconda, can greatly simplify the management of Python and deep learning dependencies.

Python, a versatile programming language, is the go-to choice for deep learning due to its extensive ecosystem of libraries and frameworks.

Deep learning frameworks like TensorFlow and PyTorch are written in Python, making it the primary language for implementing and experimenting with neural networks.

To begin, you'll need to install Python on your system.

Using a package manager like Anaconda makes this process straightforward, allowing you to create and manage isolated Python environments for different projects.

Creating a virtual environment for your deep learning work ensures that dependencies don't interfere with each other and that you have a clean slate to work with.

With Python installed, you can set up a virtual environment using commands like "conda create" or "python -m venv."

Once your virtual environment is created, you can activate it to start installing the necessary packages and libraries.

Installing essential libraries like NumPy, pandas, and Matplotlib provides a solid foundation for data manipulation and visualization in your deep learning projects.

However, the heart of any deep learning environment is the deep learning framework itself.

TensorFlow and PyTorch are the two most popular choices, with each having its unique strengths and a supportive community of users and developers.

TensorFlow, developed by Google, is known for its scalability, production-readiness, and a wide range of pre-trained models and tools.

PyTorch, on the other hand, is praised for its flexibility, dynamic computation graph, and a developer-friendly interface, making it a favorite among researchers.

To install TensorFlow, you can use the "pip" package manager with a command like "pip install tensorflow."

For PyTorch, you can visit the official website to find installation instructions tailored to your specific system and requirements.

In addition to the deep learning framework, you'll want to install GPU support libraries like CUDA for NVIDIA GPUs, as they can significantly accelerate neural network training.

Once you have your deep learning framework installed, you can test it by running a simple "Hello, World!" program to ensure that everything is functioning correctly.

You can also verify that your GPU is recognized and utilized by the framework, which is crucial for training large and complex neural networks efficiently.

Jupyter Notebook, a web-based interactive computing environment, is a valuable tool for prototyping and experimenting with deep learning models.

Installing Jupyter Notebook in your virtual environment allows you to create and run Python code in a user-friendly, browser-based interface.

With Jupyter Notebook installed, you can start a new notebook, import deep learning libraries, and begin writing and testing code cells.

Visual Studio Code (VSCode) is another popular code editor among deep learning practitioners due to its versatility and extensive extension support.

Configuring VSCode to work with your Python environment and deep learning libraries provides a convenient and efficient development environment.

Next, you'll need to acquire and preprocess data for your deep learning projects.

Datasets are the lifeblood of machine learning and deep learning, and it's essential to have a diverse set of data for experimentation.

There are various sources for datasets, including online repositories, public datasets, and data scraping tools.

Platforms like Kaggle and UCI Machine Learning Repository offer a wide range of datasets for different domains and tasks.

Preprocessing data is a critical step that involves cleaning, transforming, and organizing your data to make it suitable for training deep learning models.

This process may include tasks such as data cleaning, feature scaling, one-hot encoding, and data augmentation.

Once your data is prepared, you can begin building and training deep learning models.

Deep learning frameworks provide extensive documentation and tutorials to help you get started with creating neural networks.

You can follow these guides to build simple models and gradually progress to more complex architectures as you gain confidence and expertise.

To monitor and visualize your deep learning experiments, you can use tools like TensorBoard for TensorFlow or TensorBoardX for PyTorch.

These tools allow you to track metrics, visualize model graphs, and analyze training progress, making it easier to debug and optimize your models.

Deep learning frameworks also offer pre-trained models and transfer learning capabilities, allowing you to leverage existing architectures and weights for your own tasks.

This can save you a significant amount of time and computational resources, especially when working with limited data.

While working with deep learning models, it's crucial to experiment with different hyperparameters, architectures, and optimization techniques to find the best configuration for your specific task.

Tools like grid search and random search can help you efficiently explore the hyperparameter space and fine-tune your models.

Collaboration and sharing your work with the deep learning community can be valuable for getting feedback, learning from others, and contributing to the field.

Platforms like GitHub and GitLab provide version control and hosting for your deep learning projects, making it easy to collaborate and showcase your work.

In summary, setting up a deep learning environment involves configuring your hardware, selecting an operating system, installing Python and necessary libraries, and choosing a deep learning framework.

Once your environment is ready, you can acquire and preprocess data, build and train models, experiment with hyperparameters, and collaborate with the community to advance your deep learning skills and projects.

Chapter 7: Building and Training Neural Networks in Python

Setting up the deep learning environment is a pivotal initial step on your journey into the world of artificial intelligence and machine learning.

Before diving into the exciting realm of deep learning, you must ensure that your computing environment is appropriately configured to support the development and training of neural networks.

Your choice of hardware is fundamental, ranging from a standard laptop with a dedicated graphics processing unit (GPU) to a high-performance workstation or cloud-based virtual machine for more demanding tasks.

For many beginners, having a laptop with a GPU or access to cloud-based GPU resources is sufficient to begin learning and experimenting with deep learning.

Selecting the right operating system is crucial for your deep learning endeavors, and common choices include Windows, macOS, and various Linux distributions, with Ubuntu often being favored by researchers and developers due to its compatibility with numerous deep learning libraries and frameworks.

Additionally, installing a package manager such as Anaconda or Miniconda can simplify the management of Python and deep learning dependencies, providing a smoother experience.

Python is the primary programming language for deep learning, thanks to its extensive ecosystem of libraries and frameworks.

Frameworks like TensorFlow and PyTorch, both written in Python, are integral to implementing and experimenting with neural networks.

The installation of Python on your system is the first step towards creating a robust deep learning environment.

Using a package manager like Anaconda streamlines this process, allowing you to create and manage isolated Python environments tailored to different projects.

The creation of a virtual environment ensures that dependencies do not interfere with each other and provides a clean slate for your deep learning work.

You can create a virtual environment using commands like "conda create" or "python -m venv," tailoring it to your specific needs.

Once the virtual environment is established, activation is required to start installing the necessary packages and libraries for your deep learning journey.

Installing essential libraries like NumPy, pandas, and Matplotlib forms a solid foundation for data manipulation and visualization within your deep learning projects.

NumPy, for example, is essential for numerical operations, while pandas facilitates data manipulation and analysis, and Matplotlib supports data visualization.

However, the core of any deep learning environment lies in the choice of deep learning framework.

Two of the most popular options, TensorFlow and PyTorch, each come with unique strengths and communities of users and developers.

TensorFlow, developed by Google, is known for its scalability, production readiness, and a wide range of pre-trained models and tools.

PyTorch, on the other hand, is celebrated for its flexibility, dynamic computation graph, and user-friendly interface, making it a favorite among researchers.

To install TensorFlow, you can use the "pip" package manager with a straightforward command like "pip install tensorflow."

For PyTorch, you should visit the official website to find installation instructions customized to your system and requirements, ensuring a smooth setup process.

In addition to the deep learning framework, you'll want to install GPU support libraries like CUDA, particularly if you have an NVIDIA GPU, as they can significantly accelerate neural network training.

Verifying that your GPU is recognized and utilized by the framework is crucial for training large and complex neural networks efficiently.

Once your deep learning framework is up and running, you should perform basic tests to ensure everything is functioning correctly.

Running a simple "Hello, World!" program helps confirm that your environment is properly configured and ready for more complex tasks.

Jupyter Notebook, a web-based interactive computing environment, is an invaluable tool for prototyping and experimenting with deep learning models.

Installing Jupyter Notebook within your virtual environment allows you to create and run Python code in a user-friendly, browser-based interface.

With Jupyter Notebook at your disposal, you can start a new notebook, import deep learning libraries, and begin writing and testing code cells seamlessly.

Visual Studio Code (VSCode) is another popular code editor among deep learning practitioners due to its versatility and extensive extension support.

Configuring VSCode to work harmoniously with your Python environment and deep learning libraries provides a convenient and efficient development environment.

Once your development environment is set up, you will need to acquire and preprocess data for your deep learning projects.

Datasets form the foundation of machine learning and deep learning, so it's essential to have a diverse set of data for experimentation.

Datasets can be sourced from various places, including online repositories, public datasets, and data scraping tools.

Platforms like Kaggle and the UCI Machine Learning Repository offer a wide array of datasets spanning different domains and tasks.

Data preprocessing is a crucial step involving tasks such as data cleaning, feature scaling, one-hot encoding, and data augmentation.

These processes ensure that your data is appropriately formatted and prepared for training deep learning models, enhancing the quality of your results.

Once your data is adequately prepared, you can start building and training deep learning models.

Deep learning frameworks provide extensive documentation and tutorials to help you get started with creating neural networks.

You can follow these guides to build simple models initially and gradually progress to more complex architectures as you gain confidence and expertise.

To monitor and visualize your deep learning experiments, tools like TensorBoard for TensorFlow or TensorBoardX for PyTorch come in handy.

These tools enable you to track metrics, visualize model graphs, and analyze training progress, simplifying the debugging and optimization of your models.

Additionally, deep learning frameworks offer pre-trained models and transfer learning capabilities, enabling you to leverage existing architectures and weights for your own tasks.

This can save you a significant amount of time and computational resources, particularly when working with limited data.

While working with deep learning models, it's crucial to experiment with different hyperparameters, architectures, and optimization techniques to find the best configuration for your specific task.

Tools like grid search and random search help you efficiently explore the hyperparameter space, allowing you to fine-tune your models effectively.

Collaboration and sharing your work with the deep learning community can be highly valuable for receiving feedback, learning from others, and contributing to the field.

Platforms like GitHub and GitLab provide version control and hosting for your deep learning projects, making it easy to collaborate and showcase your work to a global audience.

In summary, setting up a deep learning environment encompasses configuring your hardware, selecting an appropriate operating system, installing Python and necessary libraries, and choosing a deep learning framework. Once your environment is prepared, you can proceed to acquire and preprocess data, build and train models, experiment with hyperparameters, and collaborate with the community to advance your deep learning skills and projects.

Building and compiling neural network models is a fundamental skill in the field of deep learning, and it is a crucial step in turning your ideas into functional and trainable networks.

When you design a neural network, you are essentially creating a computational graph that consists of interconnected layers and neurons.

These layers process and transform the input data through a series of mathematical operations, allowing the network to learn and make predictions.

To build a neural network, you'll need to select the appropriate deep learning framework you've previously set up, such as TensorFlow or PyTorch, and import the necessary libraries.

In TensorFlow, for instance, you would use commands like "import tensorflow as tf" to access the framework's functionality, while in PyTorch, "import torch" is used for the same purpose.

Once you have imported the framework, you can start defining your neural network architecture.

This involves specifying the number of layers, the type of layers, and the number of neurons in each layer.

In TensorFlow and PyTorch, you can typically create a neural network model as a class or function.

For example, in TensorFlow, you might define a class that inherits from "tf.keras.Model" and then define the layers and their connections in the class's constructor.

In PyTorch, you can create a class that inherits from "torch.nn.Module" and define the layers in the class's constructor as well.

Defining the architecture of your neural network is a critical step, as it determines the network's capacity to learn and its ability to fit the data.

Selecting the appropriate number of layers and neurons per layer depends on the complexity of your task and the amount of data available.

In general, a deep neural network with many layers and neurons can capture complex patterns but may require more data and computational resources to train effectively.

Conversely, a shallow network with fewer layers and neurons may be more suitable for simpler tasks or when computational resources are limited.

The next step in building your neural network is specifying the activation functions for each layer.

Activation functions introduce non-linearity into the network, allowing it to learn complex relationships in the data.

Common activation functions include the Rectified Linear Unit (ReLU), Sigmoid, and Hyperbolic Tangent (tanh).

In TensorFlow and PyTorch, you can typically specify the activation function when defining the layers.

For example, in TensorFlow, you can use "tf.keras.layers.ReLU()" to add a ReLU activation to a layer, while in PyTorch, "torch.nn.ReLU()" achieves the same result.

Choosing the appropriate activation function depends on the nature of your data and the specific requirements of your task.

ReLU is a popular choice due to its simplicity and effectiveness in many scenarios, but experimentation may be necessary to find the best activation function for your model.

After defining the architecture and activation functions, you need to compile your neural network model.

Compiling a model involves specifying several essential components, such as the loss function, optimizer, and evaluation metrics.

The loss function quantifies how well your model's predictions match the actual target values in your training data.

In regression tasks, Mean Squared Error (MSE) is a commonly used loss function, while in classification tasks, Cross-Entropy loss is often preferred.

In TensorFlow and PyTorch, you can select a loss function from the available options or create a custom loss function tailored to your specific task.

For example, in TensorFlow, you might use "tf.keras.losses.MeanSquaredError()" for regression or "tf.keras.losses.CategoricalCrossentropy()" for classification.

In PyTorch, you can define a custom loss function by creating a function that computes the loss based on the model's predictions and the ground truth targets.

The optimizer is another critical component of model compilation.

It determines how the model's weights are updated during training to minimize the loss function.

Common optimizers include Stochastic Gradient Descent (SGD), Adam, and RMSprop.

In TensorFlow and PyTorch, you can choose an optimizer and specify its parameters when compiling the model.

For instance, in TensorFlow, you can use "tf.keras.optimizers.SGD()" to create an SGD optimizer, while in PyTorch, "torch.optim.SGD()" serves the same purpose.

The learning rate, which controls the step size of weight updates during training, is a crucial hyperparameter to consider when choosing an optimizer.

A higher learning rate can lead to faster convergence but may risk overshooting the optimal weights, while a lower learning rate may improve convergence stability but require more training time.

Evaluating your model's performance during and after training is essential to assess its effectiveness and make necessary adjustments.

To do this, you can specify evaluation metrics when compiling the model.

In TensorFlow and PyTorch, there are predefined metrics for common tasks, such as accuracy for classification or Mean Absolute Error (MAE) for regression.

You can also create custom evaluation metrics to measure specific aspects of your model's performance.

Once you have defined the loss function, optimizer, and evaluation metrics, you can compile your neural network model by calling the "compile()" method in TensorFlow or a similar method in PyTorch.

For example, in TensorFlow, you can use "model.compile(loss='mse', optimizer='adam', metrics=['mae'])" to compile a model for regression with Mean Squared Error loss, Adam optimizer, and Mean Absolute Error as the evaluation metric.

In PyTorch, you would set up these components when defining your training loop.

After compiling your model, it's time to prepare your data for training.

You'll need to split your dataset into training, validation, and test sets to assess your model's performance on unseen data.

Data preprocessing steps, such as normalization, scaling, and one-hot encoding, should also be applied to ensure consistent and meaningful input to your model.

In TensorFlow and PyTorch, you can use data preprocessing libraries like "tf.data" and "torchvision" to efficiently prepare your data for training.

Once your data is ready, you can begin training your neural network model.

Training involves repeatedly feeding batches of data to the model, computing the loss, and updating the model's weights through backpropagation.

In TensorFlow and PyTorch, you can use built-in functions and classes to streamline the training process, such as "tf.keras.Model.fit()" in TensorFlow or custom training loops in PyTorch.

Monitoring and visualizing the training process using tools like TensorBoard or Matplotlib can help you understand how your model is learning and whether it requires adjustments.

Additionally, techniques like early stopping can prevent overfitting by monitoring validation loss and stopping training when performance starts to degrade.

Once your model has completed training, you can evaluate its performance on the test set to assess how well it generalizes to unseen data.

This step is crucial for determining the model's effectiveness in real-world applications.

In TensorFlow and PyTorch, you can use the "evaluate()" method or custom evaluation loops to measure metrics like accuracy, precision, recall, or any other relevant performance indicators.

If your model's performance is satisfactory, you can deploy it for inference in production environments.

This involves integrating your model into an application, service, or system where it can make predictions on new data.

In TensorFlow and PyTorch, you can export your trained model and use it for inference by providing input data and obtaining predictions.

Deployment considerations may vary depending on your specific use case and the platform you are targeting.

In summary, building and compiling neural network models is a multi-step process that involves defining the architecture, specifying activation functions, compiling the model with loss functions and optimizers, and setting evaluation metrics.

Once compiled, the model can be trained using training data and evaluated on a test set.

Successful deployment in real-world applications requires careful consideration of integration and deployment strategies to leverage the model's predictive capabilities effectively.

Chapter 8: Advanced Neural Network Architectures and Optimization

Advanced neural network architectures represent a significant evolution in the field of deep learning, offering enhanced capabilities for handling complex tasks and diverse types of data. These architectures include Convolutional Neural Networks (CNNs) and Recurrent Neural Networks (RNNs), each designed to address specific challenges and exploit unique data structures.

Convolutional Neural Networks, or CNNs, have revolutionized image and video analysis. They excel at tasks like image classification, object detection, and segmentation by leveraging convolutional layers to automatically learn hierarchical features from raw pixel data. In TensorFlow or PyTorch, you can create a CNN by stacking convolutional, pooling, and fully connected layers to process and interpret image data. These networks have found applications not only in traditional computer vision but also in medical image analysis, autonomous vehicles, and even natural language processing.

On the other hand, Recurrent Neural Networks, or RNNs, are tailored for sequential data processing. They are well-suited for tasks like time series prediction, speech recognition, and natural language processing. In RNNs, you can use specialized layers like Long Short-Term Memory (LSTM) or Gated Recurrent Unit (GRU) to capture temporal dependencies in the data. This allows RNNs to maintain a memory of previous inputs, making them powerful for tasks where context matters. TensorFlow and PyTorch provide built-in support for creating RNNs, making it accessible to developers.

The architectural innovations extend beyond traditional CNNs and RNNs. For example, in the field of computer vision, architectures like the U-Net have gained popularity for image segmentation tasks. U-Net is designed with an encoder-decoder structure that helps it capture fine-grained details while maintaining contextual information. Creating such architectures in TensorFlow or PyTorch often involves custom layer definitions and parameter tuning to fit the specific problem.

In natural language processing, Transformer-based architectures like BERT and GPT have achieved state-of-the-art results on various tasks. Transformers introduce a novel self-attention mechanism that allows models to consider relationships between words or tokens regardless of their positions in the input sequence. Building and training Transformers can be a complex endeavor, involving careful initialization, optimization strategies, and specialized pretraining techniques. However, these architectures have pushed the boundaries of language understanding and generation.

In some cases, hybrid models that combine CNNs, RNNs, and Transformers are becoming prevalent. These models, known as multi-modal networks, can process and extract features from different data types, such as text, images, and audio, in a unified manner. This convergence of multiple modalities allows them to perform tasks like image captioning, video analysis, or multi-modal question answering.

In the realm of reinforcement learning, neural network architectures have also evolved. Deep Q-Networks (DQNs) represent a class of neural networks used for training agents to make decisions in dynamic environments. DQNs are designed to approximate the optimal action-value function, enabling agents to learn policies for various tasks, from playing video games to autonomous navigation.

Beyond these examples, there is an ongoing effort to develop specialized neural network architectures for specific domains. For instance, graph neural networks (GNNs) are tailored for data structured as graphs, making them invaluable for tasks like social network analysis, recommendation systems, and molecular chemistry modeling.

While these advanced neural network architectures offer exciting possibilities, they come with their own set of challenges. Hyperparameter tuning, model selection, and the management of computational resources become critical considerations. Moreover, understanding the theoretical foundations and inner workings of these architectures is crucial for effectively deploying them in real-world applications.

In summary, advanced neural network architectures like CNNs, RNNs, Transformers, and their hybrid counterparts have opened up new horizons in deep learning. They have significantly expanded the scope of tasks that can be addressed with neural networks, from image and speech processing to natural language understanding and reinforcement learning. However, harnessing their power requires a deep understanding of their underlying principles and careful engineering to tailor them to specific applications. As the field continues to evolve, these architectures are likely to play a pivotal role in the advancement of artificial intelligence and machine learning.

Optimization techniques and learning rate schedules are critical components of training neural networks, as they govern the process of updating model weights to minimize the loss function effectively. These techniques are crucial for ensuring that your model converges to a good solution while avoiding common pitfalls like slow convergence or divergence.

One of the most widely used optimization techniques is Stochastic Gradient Descent (SGD), a variant of gradient descent. It works by iteratively updating the model's weights based on the gradient of the loss with respect to those weights. In TensorFlow or PyTorch, you can instantiate an SGD optimizer with a specified learning rate using commands like "tf.keras.optimizers.SGD()" or "torch.optim.SGD()".

The learning rate is a hyperparameter that controls the step size during weight updates. Setting the right learning rate is essential because a too-small rate may lead to slow convergence, while a too-large rate may result in overshooting the optimal weights and divergence. Experimentation and learning rate schedules can help determine the appropriate value. Learning rate schedules adjust the learning rate during training. These schedules can be either fixed or dynamic, and they can greatly influence the training process. Fixed schedules keep the learning rate constant throughout training, while dynamic schedules change it at specific intervals. In TensorFlow or PyTorch, you can implement a dynamic learning rate schedule by defining a learning rate callback or using built-in functions like "tf.keras.optimizers.schedules" or "torch.optim.lr_scheduler".

One common dynamic schedule is the learning rate decay, where the learning rate decreases gradually over time. This approach can help the model converge faster in the initial stages when larger updates are necessary, while reducing the risk of overshooting in later stages. Another popular schedule is the learning rate annealing, where the learning rate is reduced by a fixed factor after a certain number of epochs. This method allows for more fine-grained control over the learning rate decay rate.

Additionally, techniques like the learning rate warm-up involve starting with a small learning rate and gradually increasing it in the early training stages. This can help the model explore a wider range of solutions before settling into a narrow basin. Learning rate schedules can be tailored to the specific needs of your model and problem domain. For instance, in natural language processing tasks, models like Transformers often benefit from specialized schedules like the "transformer learning rate schedule," which adjusts the learning rate differently for different parts of the model.

Another optimization technique worth mentioning is momentum. Momentum helps accelerate SGD by accumulating a moving average of gradients. This technique allows the optimizer to maintain a sense of direction and reduce oscillations, improving convergence speed and stability. In TensorFlow and PyTorch, you can incorporate momentum into your optimizer by specifying the momentum parameter when creating an instance of SGD.

An extension of momentum is the Nesterov Accelerated Gradient (NAG), which computes gradients with respect to the moving average of weights. This approach can lead to even faster convergence, especially in deep networks. Implementing NAG in TensorFlow or PyTorch is straightforward, as it often requires only a minor modification to the optimizer setup.

In addition to traditional optimization techniques, modern deep learning libraries provide access to a variety of advanced optimizers, such as Adam, RMSprop, and AdaGrad. These optimizers incorporate adaptive learning rates and momentum-like components to improve convergence in various scenarios. You can use these optimizers in

TensorFlow or PyTorch with simple commands like "tf.keras.optimizers.Adam()" or "torch.optim.Adam()".

Furthermore, techniques like batch normalization, weight decay (L2 regularization), and dropout can aid in optimization by improving the stability of training and preventing overfitting. Batch normalization normalizes activations within each mini-batch, reducing internal covariate shift and allowing for more stable gradient updates. Weight decay adds a regularization term to the loss function, penalizing large weights and encouraging the model to generalize better. Dropout randomly deactivates neurons during training, preventing overfitting by reducing the model's reliance on specific neurons.

To effectively use these optimization techniques and learning rate schedules, it's essential to monitor and evaluate your model's training progress. Tools like TensorBoard or custom monitoring scripts can help you visualize training curves, including loss and accuracy over time. Regularly inspecting these metrics can guide your decisions on whether to adjust the learning rate or try different optimization strategies.

In summary, optimization techniques and learning rate schedules are pivotal in training neural networks effectively. Techniques like SGD, momentum, and Nesterov Accelerated Gradient, combined with appropriate learning rate schedules, help models converge faster and achieve better results. The choice of optimizer and schedule depends on the problem domain and the specific characteristics of your data. Experimentation and continuous monitoring of training progress are essential for finding the optimal combination and ensuring successful model training.

Chapter 9: Transfer Learning and Model Deployment

Leveraging pretrained models and knowledge transfer is a powerful strategy in deep learning that can save you time and resources while improving the performance of your models. Pretrained models are neural networks that have been trained on large datasets for specific tasks, such as image classification, object detection, or natural language processing. These models have learned valuable features and representations that can be reused for related tasks, making them a valuable resource for both beginners and experts in the field.

In TensorFlow or PyTorch, loading pretrained models is often as simple as using a command like "tf.keras.applications.MobileNetV2()" or "torchvision.models.resnet18(pretrained=True)". These commands download the pre-trained model weights and architecture, allowing you to use them as a starting point for your specific task.

One common use case for pretrained models is transfer learning. Transfer learning involves taking a pretrained model and fine-tuning it on a smaller, domain-specific dataset. This process can be particularly beneficial when you have limited labeled data or want to adapt a model to a different but related task. By initializing your model with pretrained weights, you can leverage the knowledge the model has already acquired, often achieving faster convergence and better performance.

For example, if you're working on an image classification task for a specific set of animals and have access to a pretrained model like ResNet or MobileNet, you can start with the pretrained weights and fine-tune the model on your dataset.

The lower layers of the model have already learned basic features like edges, textures, and shapes, which are likely relevant to your new task. Fine-tuning allows the model to adjust its higher-level features to match the specific characteristics of your data.

In natural language processing, pretrained language models like BERT or GPT-3 have gained significant attention. These models have been trained on massive text corpora and can be fine-tuned for various NLP tasks, such as sentiment analysis, text classification, or named entity recognition. By using these pretrained language models as a foundation, you can build and fine-tune models that excel at understanding and generating human language.

When fine-tuning pretrained models, it's essential to consider the architecture and hyperparameters carefully. You may need to adjust the learning rate, batch size, and other training parameters to ensure the model adapts effectively to your data. Also, monitoring the training progress and evaluating performance on validation data is crucial to prevent overfitting and achieve the best results.

Another approach to knowledge transfer is feature extraction. In this technique, you use the pretrained model as a fixed feature extractor, removing the final classification layer and using the output from the layer just before it as the feature representation. You can then train a new classifier on top of these fixed features for your specific task. This approach is beneficial when you have limited computational resources or want to extract features for multiple tasks efficiently.

For example, if you have a pretrained image classification model, you can remove the last fully connected layer and use the output from the previous layer as feature vectors. These feature vectors can serve as input to a new classifier, such as a support vector machine or a simple feedforward neural network, for a different classification task, like detecting specific objects or diseases in medical images.

Pretrained models are not limited to vision and natural language processing domains; they also exist for tasks like speech recognition, audio analysis, recommendation systems, and more. These models have been fine-tuned on vast datasets and have learned valuable representations that can significantly boost your model's performance, even if you have limited data.

Furthermore, you can combine multiple pretrained models and transfer knowledge across modalities. For instance, you can use a pretrained vision model's features as input to a language model for tasks that require understanding both text and images, like image captioning or visual question answering.

It's essential to acknowledge that while pretrained models offer numerous advantages, they might not always be the best choice. If your task is vastly different from the one the model was pretrained on, it may be more beneficial to start from scratch or use a smaller, domain-specific architecture. Additionally, pretrained models can be computationally intensive, so you should consider your hardware and resource constraints.

In summary, leveraging pretrained models and knowledge transfer is a valuable strategy in deep learning. Pretrained models, whether in computer vision, natural language processing, or other domains, offer a significant head start in model development. Transfer learning and feature extraction allow you to adapt these models to specific tasks efficiently. However, careful consideration of architecture, hyperparameters, and evaluation is necessary to ensure the best results for your particular use case. As pretrained models continue to advance, they will remain a fundamental tool for both beginners and experts in the field of deep learning.

Deploying machine learning models in real-world applications is a critical and often challenging step in the machine learning pipeline. It involves taking a trained model and making it accessible for use in production systems, where it can provide valuable insights or predictions. This process requires careful planning, infrastructure setup, and considerations for scalability, security, and reliability.

One of the first steps in deploying a machine learning model is choosing the right deployment platform. Popular options include cloud-based platforms like Amazon Web Services (AWS), Google Cloud Platform (GCP), Microsoft Azure, or container orchestration platforms like Kubernetes. These platforms offer a range of services and tools that can simplify the deployment process, including managed machine learning services.

Once you have chosen a deployment platform, the next step is to prepare your model for deployment. This often involves converting the model into a format that can be easily loaded and used by your production environment. Common formats for model deployment include TensorFlow's SavedModel format, ONNX (Open Neural Network Exchange), or a custom format that suits your needs. You can use commands like "tensorflow.saved_model.save()" to save a model in the TensorFlow format or "onnx.export()" for ONNX.

Scalability is a crucial consideration when deploying machine learning models in real-world applications. You need to ensure that your deployed model can handle varying workloads and adapt to changes in demand. This often involves setting up auto-scaling capabilities that can dynamically allocate resources based on traffic. Platforms like Kubernetes provide built-in support for auto-scaling based on metrics like CPU or memory usage.

In addition to scalability, security is a paramount concern when deploying machine learning models. You must protect your models, data, and infrastructure from potential threats and unauthorized access. Implementing security best practices, such as encryption, access controls, and authentication mechanisms, is essential. Commands like "kubectl create secret" in Kubernetes can be used to manage sensitive information like API keys securely.

Reliability is another critical aspect of deploying machine learning models. Production systems must be designed to handle failures gracefully and ensure high availability. This includes setting up redundancy, monitoring systems, and automated recovery procedures. Platforms like AWS offer services like Amazon Elastic Load Balancing (ELB) and Amazon CloudWatch for monitoring and managing the reliability of deployed models.

Once your model is deployed, it's essential to monitor its performance in real-time. Monitoring allows you to detect issues, track usage, and gather insights into how your model is behaving in production. Tools like Prometheus and Grafana can be used for collecting and visualizing metrics, while log aggregators like Elasticsearch and Kibana can help you track and analyze logs.

Continuous integration and continuous deployment (CI/CD) pipelines are invaluable for maintaining and updating deployed models. These pipelines automate the process of testing and deploying new versions of your model, ensuring that changes are thoroughly validated before reaching production. Commands like "git push" and CI/CD tools like

Jenkins or GitLab CI/CD can be integrated into your workflow to streamline this process.

To make machine learning models accessible to users or other systems, you'll often need to expose them through APIs (Application Programming Interfaces). APIs allow external applications to send requests to your model and receive predictions or responses. Web frameworks like Flask or FastAPI can be used to create RESTful APIs that wrap your model's functionality, making it easy for clients to interact with the model.

Model versioning is crucial when deploying machine learning models in real-world applications. You need a system that can keep track of different versions of your model, allowing you to roll back to previous versions if issues arise with new deployments. Git or dedicated versioning tools can help manage model versions effectively.

To ensure that your deployed model remains accurate and relevant, you may need to implement a feedback loop that collects user feedback and uses it to retrain the model periodically. This involves updating your training data, retraining the model, and deploying the new version. Command-line tools like "git merge" and automated pipelines can facilitate this process.

Lastly, documentation is essential for anyone interacting with your deployed model, from developers integrating the API to data scientists retraining the model. Clear and comprehensive documentation should explain the API endpoints, input and output formats, and any specific requirements or constraints.

In summary, deploying machine learning models in real-world applications is a multifaceted process that requires careful planning, infrastructure setup, and considerations for scalability, security, reliability, and more. Leveraging the right deployment platform, preparing your model for deployment, monitoring its performance, and maintaining a CI/CD pipeline are essential steps. Ensuring security, reliability, and version control while exposing your model through APIs and maintaining documentation are key aspects of successful model deployment in production systems.

Chapter 10: Solving Real-World Problems with Python Machine Learning

Case studies and practical applications provide valuable insights into how machine learning and deep learning techniques are applied in real-world scenarios. These real-world examples illustrate the versatility and impact of these technologies across various domains and industries. By examining specific cases and practical applications, we can gain a deeper understanding of the challenges, solutions, and outcomes achieved through the use of machine learning and deep learning.

One notable case study in the healthcare industry involves the use of deep learning for medical image analysis. Deep neural networks have shown remarkable performance in tasks such as diagnosing diseases from medical images like X-rays, CT scans, and MRI scans. By utilizing convolutional neural networks (CNNs) and training them on vast datasets of medical images, researchers and healthcare professionals can automate disease detection and improve diagnostic accuracy.

For example, deep learning models have been deployed to detect and classify various forms of cancer, including breast cancer and lung cancer, from medical images. These models can analyze mammograms and chest X-rays, identify suspicious lesions or anomalies, and provide early alerts to medical practitioners. This has the potential to significantly enhance the speed and accuracy of cancer diagnosis, leading to earlier interventions and improved patient outcomes.

Another intriguing application of machine learning is in the field of autonomous vehicles and self-driving cars. Self-driving cars rely on a combination of sensors, cameras, and machine learning algorithms to perceive their environment and make real-time driving decisions. Reinforcement learning is often used to train autonomous vehicles to navigate complex road scenarios.

Command: "python train_reinforcement_learning_agent.py"

In this context, case studies involve testing self-driving cars in diverse environments, including urban, suburban, and highway settings. These studies examine how machine learning models adapt to different driving conditions, handle unexpected obstacles, and ensure passenger safety. The ultimate goal is to develop autonomous vehicles that can reduce accidents, improve traffic flow, and provide efficient transportation solutions.

Moving beyond healthcare and transportation, machine learning has found applications in the finance industry. Financial institutions use machine learning algorithms for fraud detection, credit risk assessment, and algorithmic trading. These algorithms analyze vast amounts of financial data to identify fraudulent transactions, evaluate borrowers' creditworthiness, and make data-driven investment decisions.

For instance, in credit risk assessment, banks use historical financial data and machine learning models to predict the likelihood of a borrower defaulting on a loan. By analyzing variables such as income, credit history, and economic indicators, these models can assess credit risk more accurately than traditional methods. This reduces the chance of lending to high-risk borrowers and minimizes financial losses for banks.

Command: "run_credit_risk_prediction.py"

Another practical application of machine learning is in natural language processing (NLP). NLP models, such as transformer-based architectures like BERT and GPT-3, have revolutionized how we interact with text and language.

These models can perform tasks like sentiment analysis, text summarization, language translation, and chatbot development.

Case studies in NLP involve the development of chatbots for customer support in various industries. These chatbots utilize machine learning models to understand and respond to customer queries and requests. By analyzing customer interactions and continuously improving their language understanding capabilities, chatbots can provide efficient and personalized customer service.

Command: "python train_chatbot.py"

Furthermore, machine learning plays a vital role in recommendation systems, which are used by online platforms like e-commerce websites and streaming services to suggest products or content to users. Recommendation systems leverage collaborative filtering, content-based filtering, and deep learning techniques to understand user preferences and make personalized recommendations.

In the context of e-commerce, case studies involve improving the accuracy of product recommendations to increase user engagement and sales. Machine learning models are trained on historical user behavior data, such as browsing and purchase history, to predict which products a user is likely to be interested in. By tailoring recommendations to individual users, e-commerce platforms can enhance the shopping experience and drive revenue growth.

Command: "python train_recommendation_model.py"

In the field of computer vision, practical applications extend beyond healthcare to areas like agriculture and manufacturing. For example, drones equipped with cameras and machine learning algorithms are used in precision agriculture to monitor crop health, detect pests or diseases, and optimize irrigation. By analyzing aerial images and providing actionable insights to farmers, these systems can improve crop yields and reduce resource wastage.

Command: "run_precision_agriculture_drone.py"

In manufacturing, computer vision is applied to quality control and defect detection. Machine learning models can analyze images of products on assembly lines to identify defects, ensuring that only high-quality products reach consumers. This improves product quality, reduces manufacturing costs, and enhances customer satisfaction.

Command: "run_quality_control_inspection.py"

These case studies and practical applications highlight the diverse range of industries and domains where machine learning and deep learning are making a significant impact. From healthcare to transportation, finance to natural language processing, and computer vision to recommendation systems, these technologies are driving innovation, solving complex problems, and transforming how businesses and organizations operate. The real-world success stories presented in these examples underscore the potential for machine learning and deep learning to bring about positive change and drive progress in our increasingly data-driven world.

As we explore the ever-evolving landscape of machine learning, it's essential to acknowledge the challenges that researchers, practitioners, and the field as a whole face. These challenges drive innovation, shape the future of machine learning, and pave the way for exciting developments. Next, we'll delve into some of the most pressing challenges and discuss the potential future directions of this dynamic field.

Command: "python explore_challenges.py"

One of the primary challenges in machine learning is the need for vast amounts of high-quality labeled data. Many machine learning algorithms, particularly deep learning models, rely on large datasets to achieve high levels of performance. Collecting and annotating such datasets can be expensive and time-consuming, limiting the accessibility of machine learning to smaller organizations and projects.

Addressing this challenge involves exploring techniques for efficient data labeling, data augmentation, and the development of semi-supervised or unsupervised learning approaches. Additionally, ongoing research in transfer learning, where models pretrained on one task are fine-tuned for another, can help reduce the data requirements for specific applications.

Command: "python explore_data_labeling_techniques.py"

Another significant challenge is the interpretability and explainability of machine learning models. While complex models like deep neural networks often achieve state-of-the-art results, they can be difficult to understand, leading to concerns about their reliability and fairness. Interpretable models are crucial, especially in high-stakes domains like healthcare and finance, where model decisions can have profound consequences.

To address this challenge, researchers are developing techniques to explain model predictions, such as feature importance scores, attention mechanisms, and rule-based explanations. Future directions may involve creating more interpretable model architectures or exploring the trade-offs between model complexity and interpretability.

Command: "python explore_interpretability_methods.py"

Ethics, bias, and fairness are becoming increasingly important considerations in machine learning. Biases present in training data can lead to biased model predictions, resulting in unfair outcomes for certain groups. Detecting and mitigating bias in machine learning models is a complex challenge that requires careful attention and ongoing research.

Commands: "python assess_bias_in_model.py" and "python mitigate_bias_in_model.py"

To promote fairness and address bias, future directions in machine learning include the development of fairness-aware algorithms, the establishment of ethical guidelines, and the incorporation of diverse perspectives in the machine learning community. Ensuring that machine learning models are transparent, accountable, and equitable is essential for building trust and ensuring the responsible deployment of AI technologies.

The scalability of machine learning models is another significant challenge, especially in the context of deep learning. As models grow in size and complexity, training and deploying them become computationally intensive tasks. This can lead to increased energy consumption and environmental concerns, as well as accessibility issues for organizations with limited computational resources.

Command: "python assess_model_scalability.py"

Future directions in addressing scalability challenges may involve the development of more efficient model architectures, the optimization of hardware and software infrastructure for machine learning tasks, and the exploration of federated learning and edge computing to distribute model training and inference.

The robustness and security of machine learning models are also areas of concern. Adversarial attacks, where malicious actors attempt to manipulate model predictions by making subtle changes to input data, can undermine the reliability of machine learning systems. Ensuring the resilience of models against such attacks is a critical challenge.

Commands: "python assess_model_robustness.py" and "python enhance_model_security.py"

Future directions for addressing security challenges may involve the development of adversarial training techniques, the incorporation of robustness checks during model evaluation, and research into secure and privacy-preserving machine learning methods.

While these challenges are complex and multifaceted, they offer exciting opportunities for innovation and advancement in the field of machine learning. Researchers and practitioners continue to push the boundaries of what is possible, working towards solutions that can make machine learning more accessible, interpretable, ethical, fair, scalable, robust, and secure.

As we look ahead to the future of machine learning, we can anticipate several key directions that will shape the field. One of these directions is the ongoing development of specialized hardware accelerators tailored for machine learning workloads. These accelerators, such as GPUs and TPUs, have played a pivotal role in the rapid advancement of deep learning. Future hardware innovations are expected to further optimize model training and inference, making machine learning more efficient and accessible.

Command: "python explore_specialized_hardware.py"

Another direction is the exploration of novel model architectures beyond deep learning. While deep neural networks have achieved remarkable results, they are not the only approach to machine learning. Future research may focus on innovative model architectures inspired by biological systems, quantum computing, or other paradigms, opening up new possibilities for solving complex problems.

Command: "python explore_novel_model_architectures.py"

Federated learning is poised to become a prominent direction in machine learning. This approach allows multiple parties to collaborate on model training without sharing their raw data. Federated learning can enhance privacy and security while enabling the development of global models that benefit from decentralized data sources.

Command: "python explore_federated_learning.py"

Explainable AI (XAI) will continue to gain importance as the demand for transparent and interpretable machine learning models grows. Future research will likely focus on improving XAI techniques, making them more accessible and applicable across various domains.

Command: "python explore_future_xai_techniques.py"

Machine learning will also play a pivotal role in addressing critical global challenges, such as climate change, healthcare, and sustainability. Future applications may include climate modeling, drug discovery, and optimizing resource allocation to reduce environmental impact.

Command: "python explore_machine_learning_global_challenges.py"

The convergence of machine learning with other fields, such as robotics, neuroscience, and materials science, will lead to interdisciplinary breakthroughs. These collaborations will drive innovation in areas like autonomous robotics, brain-computer interfaces, and materials discovery.

Command: "python explore_interdisciplinary_machine_learning.py"

The democratization of machine learning tools and knowledge will continue to expand access to AI technologies. Open-source frameworks, online courses, and collaborative platforms will empower individuals and organizations to leverage machine learning for their specific needs.

Command: "python explore_democratization_of_machine_learning.py"

In summary, the challenges and future directions in machine learning are intertwined, with each challenge presenting an opportunity for future progress. As the field evolves, researchers, practitioners, and the broader community will collaborate to overcome these challenges and drive innovation. The future of machine learning holds promise for addressing complex problems, enhancing our understanding of AI systems, and delivering transformative solutions across diverse domains.

BOOK 4
ADVANCED DEEP LEARNING
CUTTING-EDGE TECHNIQUES AND APPLICATIONS

ROB BOTWRIGHT

Chapter 1: The Evolving Landscape of Deep Learning

The journey of deep learning is marked by a series of remarkable milestones that have shaped the landscape of artificial intelligence. These milestones reflect the persistent pursuit of human-level intelligence in machines and the groundbreaking innovations that have brought us closer to that goal.

Command: "python explore_deep_learning_history.py"

One of the early milestones in the history of deep learning dates back to 1943 when Warren McCulloch and Walter Pitts introduced the concept of artificial neurons in their seminal paper "A Logical Calculus of the Ideas Immanent in Nervous Activity." This theoretical framework laid the foundation for neural networks and inspired subsequent developments in the field.

Command: "python explore_mcculloch_pitts_neuron.py"

The term "artificial intelligence" was coined in 1956 during the Dartmouth Workshop, a seminal event that gathered leading researchers to explore the possibilities of machine intelligence. Although the term initially generated significant enthusiasm, progress in AI faced challenges that would become evident in the following decades.

Command: "python explore_dartmouth_workshop.py"

In the 1960s and 1970s, AI research focused on symbolic reasoning and expert systems. This period witnessed significant achievements, such as the development of expert systems like Dendral and MYCIN, which demonstrated the potential of AI for knowledge-based tasks.

Command: "python explore_expert_systems.py"

However, the limitations of symbolic AI became apparent as it struggled to handle uncertainty, learn from data, and perform tasks that required perception and understanding of the real world. This led to what is often referred to as the "AI winter," a period of reduced funding and enthusiasm for AI research.

Command: "python explore_ai_winter.py"

The resurgence of neural networks and deep learning occurred in the 1980s, marked by the work of researchers like Geoffrey Hinton, Yann LeCun, and Yoshua Bengio. Hinton's pioneering work on backpropagation and LeCun's development of convolutional neural networks (CNNs) were crucial contributions during this time.

Command: "python explore_neural_network_resurgence.py"

Despite these advances, deep learning faced challenges related to training deep networks effectively, often referred to as the "vanishing gradient" problem. The field made progress, but it had not yet reached the level of performance and scalability that would lead to its widespread adoption.

Command: "python explore_vanishing_gradient_problem.py"

The breakthrough moment for deep learning came with the advent of powerful hardware, particularly graphics processing units (GPUs), which accelerated neural network training. This hardware revolution, combined with large datasets and innovative algorithms, led to significant improvements in the performance of deep neural networks.

Command: "python explore_gpu_acceleration.py"

In 2012, a pivotal moment occurred when a deep convolutional neural network named AlexNet won the ImageNet Large Scale Visual Recognition Challenge. AlexNet demonstrated a remarkable reduction in image classification error rates, reigniting interest in deep learning and setting the stage for its dominance in computer vision tasks.

Command: "python explore_alexnet_and_imagenet.py"

The years that followed saw a rapid expansion of deep learning into various domains, including natural language processing, speech recognition, and reinforcement learning. Key milestones included the success of recurrent neural networks (RNNs) in language modeling and the development of deep reinforcement learning algorithms.

Command: "python explore_deep_learning_expansion.py"

The availability of open-source deep learning frameworks, such as TensorFlow and PyTorch, played a crucial role in democratizing the field. These frameworks made it easier for researchers and practitioners to build, train, and deploy deep neural networks, fostering collaboration and innovation.

Command: "python explore_open_source_frameworks.py"

The AlphaGo victory by DeepMind in 2016 demonstrated the potential of deep reinforcement learning in complex strategic games. AlphaGo's ability to defeat world champion Go players marked a significant milestone in AI research and captured global attention.

Command: "python explore_alphago_victory.py"

As deep learning continued to advance, it found applications in healthcare, autonomous vehicles, finance, and many other industries. Deep learning models became integral to medical image analysis, autonomous driving systems, and financial forecasting.

Command: "python explore_deep_learning_applications.py"

The pursuit of artificial general intelligence (AGI), or human-level AI, remains an overarching goal in deep learning. Researchers are exploring novel architectures, such as transformers and neural networks inspired by the brain's structure, in the quest for more capable and versatile AI systems.

Command: "python explore_pursuit_of_artificial_general_intelligence.py"

In summary, the historical milestones in deep learning reflect a journey marked by persistence, innovation, and collaboration. From the early theoretical foundations to the modern applications, deep learning has transformed the field of artificial intelligence and continues to shape the future of AI research and technology.

In recent years, the field of deep learning has experienced a flurry of groundbreaking research and exciting trends. These advancements have propelled artificial intelligence to new heights and opened up a world of possibilities for applications across various domains.
Command: "python explore_deep_learning_trends.py"
One notable trend is the evolution of transformer-based models, which have revolutionized natural language processing (NLP). Transformers, first introduced in the landmark paper "Attention Is All You Need" by Vaswani et al. in 2017, have become the backbone of state-of-the-art NLP models.
Command: "python explore_transformer_models.py"
The development of models like BERT (Bidirectional Encoder Representations from Transformers) and GPT (Generative Pretrained Transformer) has enabled machines to understand and generate human-like text at unprecedented levels. These models have applications in sentiment analysis, language translation, and question-answering systems.
Command: "python explore_bert_and_gpt.py"
Another significant advancement in deep learning is the emergence of self-supervised learning. This paradigm shift allows models to learn from unlabeled data, making it more scalable and accessible. Self-supervised learning has been instrumental in improving the performance of various tasks, including image and speech recognition.
Command: "python explore_self_supervised_learning.py"

The integration of deep learning into healthcare has garnered immense attention, especially in medical image analysis and disease diagnosis. Deep neural networks have demonstrated their ability to detect anomalies in medical images with high accuracy, aiding radiologists and doctors in early disease detection.

Command: "python explore_deep_learning_in_healthcare.py"

Reinforcement learning, a subfield of deep learning, has seen notable advancements in training agents to excel in complex tasks. AlphaZero, developed by DeepMind, mastered chess, shogi, and Go without human knowledge, showcasing the potential of reinforcement learning in strategic games and decision-making scenarios.

Command: "python explore_alpha_zero.py"

The fusion of deep learning and computer vision has led to remarkable breakthroughs in object detection and image segmentation. Models like YOLO (You Only Look Once) and Mask R-CNN have made real-time object detection and pixel-level image segmentation achievable in applications like autonomous driving and medical imaging.

Command: "python explore_object_detection_and_segmentation.py"

Ethical considerations in AI and deep learning have become increasingly important. Researchers and practitioners are actively addressing issues related to bias, fairness, and transparency in AI systems. Ethical AI frameworks and guidelines are being developed to ensure responsible and equitable use of AI technologies.

Command: "python explore_ethical_ai_in_deep_learning.py"

Quantum computing and deep learning are converging to explore new frontiers. Quantum neural networks and quantum-inspired algorithms are being developed to harness the power of quantum computing for tasks like optimization and data analysis. These efforts could potentially revolutionize deep learning in the future.

Command: "python explore_quantum_computing_and_deep_learning.py"

Interpretable AI and explainable deep learning are critical areas of research to enhance the trustworthiness of AI systems. Techniques that provide insights into model decisions are essential for applications where transparency is paramount, such as healthcare and autonomous vehicles.

Command: "python explore_interpretable_ai.py"

The democratization of AI is another notable trend. Open-source deep learning frameworks, extensive online courses, and prebuilt models have made it easier for individuals and organizations to engage in AI research and development. This democratization is fostering innovation and collaboration across the global AI community.

Command: "python explore_democratization_of_ai.py"

In summary, recent advances and trends in deep learning are shaping the future of artificial intelligence. From transformer-based NLP models to self-supervised learning and ethical considerations, the field continues to evolve, offering exciting opportunities and challenges. Deep learning's influence extends across industries, paving the way for more intelligent and capable AI systems that will transform our world.

Chapter 2: Generative Adversarial Networks (GANs) and Variational Autoencoders (VAEs)

Generative Adversarial Networks, commonly referred to as GANs, have emerged as a groundbreaking concept in the field of deep learning. GANs were introduced by Ian Goodfellow and his colleagues in 2014 and have since become one of the most exciting and widely researched areas of artificial intelligence.
Command: "python explore_gans_intro.py"
At the heart of GANs is the idea of generating data, whether it be images, text, or any other type of information. What makes GANs particularly fascinating is their ability to create data that is almost indistinguishable from real data, often leading to photorealistic images and coherent text generation.
Command: "python explore_gans_data_generation.py"
The fundamental architecture of a GAN consists of two neural networks: the generator and the discriminator. These networks are in a constant adversarial relationship, hence the name "Generative Adversarial Networks." The generator's role is to create data, while the discriminator's task is to distinguish between real and generated data.
Command: "python explore_gans_architecture.py"
The training process of GANs can be likened to a cat-and-mouse game between the generator and discriminator. The generator starts with random noise as input and attempts to generate data that is as close to real data as possible. Simultaneously, the discriminator is trying to improve its ability to differentiate real from fake data.
Command: "python explore_gans_training_process.py"

The adversarial nature of GANs leads to a continuous feedback loop, where the generator becomes better at generating data as the discriminator becomes more skilled at detecting fake data. This competitive process drives the improvement of both networks over time.
Command: "python explore_gans_feedback_loop.py"
One of the early successes of GANs was in the domain of image generation. Researchers demonstrated that GANs could generate high-quality images of faces, animals, and various objects. This breakthrough opened up possibilities for applications in art, design, and even image synthesis for medical research.
Command: "python explore_gans_image_generation.py"
GANs have also been applied to style transfer, where the style of one image can be applied to another. This technique has found applications in creating artistic filters, transforming photos into famous painting styles, and enhancing the aesthetics of images.
Command: "python explore_gans_style_transfer.py"
Text generation using GANs has made significant strides. Language models like GPT-3, based on the transformer architecture, have demonstrated the ability to generate coherent and contextually relevant text. This has found applications in chatbots, content generation, and even writing assistance.
Command: "python explore_gans_text_generation.py"
Conditional GANs introduced the concept of controlling the generated output by providing additional information to the generator. For example, by conditioning a GAN on specific attributes, you can generate images of a particular class or style, making GANs even more versatile.
Command: "python explore_conditional_gans.py"
Despite their remarkable successes, GANs have faced challenges, such as mode collapse, where the generator

produces a limited set of outputs, and training stability issues. Researchers continue to explore ways to mitigate these challenges and improve the training dynamics of GANs.

Command: "python explore_gans_challenges.py"

The applications of GANs extend beyond art and entertainment. GANs have been used in medical imaging to generate synthetic data for training machine learning models and improving the diagnosis of diseases. They have also found applications in creating realistic synthetic data for various industries, such as autonomous vehicles and robotics.

Command: "python explore_gans_applications.py"

Ethical considerations in GANs are crucial, especially concerning the generation of deepfakes, where GANs can be used to create convincing but fake videos and images of individuals. The misuse of GANs for malicious purposes has raised concerns about privacy and misinformation.

Command: "python explore_ethical_issues_in_gans.py"

In summary, Generative Adversarial Networks have revolutionized the field of deep learning and artificial intelligence. Their ability to generate realistic data has opened up new horizons in art, design, text generation, and numerous other applications. As GANs continue to evolve, researchers and practitioners must navigate the ethical challenges and harness the potential for positive impact on various industries and domains.

Variational Autoencoders, often abbreviated as VAEs, are a type of generative model that have gained significant attention in the field of deep learning. VAEs are particularly noteworthy for their ability to generate new data samples that closely resemble the training data, making them valuable for various applications.

Command: "python explore_vae_intro.py"
The concept of autoencoders, the foundation of VAEs, dates back to the early days of neural networks. Autoencoders are neural networks designed to learn efficient representations of input data by encoding it into a lower-dimensional latent space and then decoding it back to its original form.
Command: "python explore_autoencoders.py"
Variational Autoencoders, introduced by Kingma and Welling in 2013, add a probabilistic twist to traditional autoencoders. Instead of directly encoding data into a fixed latent representation, VAEs model the latent space as a probability distribution, typically a Gaussian distribution.
Command: "python explore_vae_probability_distribution.py"
The key innovation in VAEs is the introduction of two essential components: the encoder and the decoder. The encoder maps input data to the parameters of the latent space's probability distribution, while the decoder samples from this distribution and reconstructs the data.
Command: "python explore_vae_encoder_decoder.py"
By modeling the latent space as a probability distribution, VAEs enable the generation of data samples that follow a coherent and structured pattern. This stochasticity in the latent space contributes to the diversity of generated samples.
Command: "python explore_vae_stochasticity.py"
One of the advantages of VAEs is their capability to generate data that resembles the training data while also allowing for smooth interpolation between data points in the latent space. This interpolation property is useful for tasks like image editing and style transfer.
Command: "python explore_vae_interpolation.py"
In training VAEs, the objective is to optimize a loss function that encourages the learned latent space to follow a

standard Gaussian distribution. This loss function consists of two parts: a reconstruction loss, which measures how well the data is reconstructed, and a regularization term called the Kullback-Leibler (KL) divergence.

Command: "python explore_vae_loss_function.py"

Variational Autoencoders find applications in various domains, including image generation, data denoising, and anomaly detection. For example, VAEs have been used to generate realistic faces, objects, and even artistic images.

Command: "python explore_vae_applications.py"

In the context of semi-supervised learning, VAEs can be employed to improve the performance of models when labeled data is scarce. They do this by learning a meaningful latent representation that captures underlying data structures.

Command: "python explore_vae_semi_supervised_learning.py"

VAEs also play a crucial role in generative modeling of sequential data, such as text and music. Recurrent Variational Autoencoders (RVAEs) extend the VAE framework to handle sequential data, enabling the generation of coherent text and music compositions.

Command: "python explore_rvae_text_generation.py"

The interpretability of VAEs is an ongoing research area. Understanding and controlling the generative process in VAEs is essential, especially in applications where data generation should adhere to specific constraints and semantics.

Command: "python explore_vae_interpretability.py"

Like other generative models, ethical considerations come into play with VAEs, particularly in generating realistic but fake data. The potential misuse of VAEs for creating deepfakes and spreading misinformation underscores the importance of responsible AI usage.

Command: "python explore_ethical_issues_in_vaes.py"
In summary, Variational Autoencoders have made significant contributions to the field of generative modeling. Their probabilistic framework, ability to generate structured data, and versatility in various domains make them a valuable tool in data generation and semi-supervised learning. However, as with any AI technology, ethical considerations must guide their use to ensure responsible and ethical applications.

Chapter 3: Transformers and Attention Mechanisms

Attention mechanisms have become a fundamental component in deep learning models, transforming how neural networks process information and handle complex tasks. These mechanisms, inspired by human cognitive processes, have found widespread applications in natural language processing, computer vision, and various other fields of artificial intelligence.

Command: "python explore_attention_intro.py"

The concept of attention in deep learning draws inspiration from selective perception in humans, where focus is directed towards specific elements of a task while ignoring irrelevant information. Attention mechanisms aim to replicate this selective processing in neural networks, enhancing their ability to analyze and generate meaningful information.

Command: "python explore_attention_human_inspiration.py"

The inception of attention mechanisms can be traced back to the introduction of recurrent neural networks (RNNs), where they were initially used to weigh different parts of input sequences when making predictions. However, the true breakthrough occurred with the development of the transformer architecture.

Command: "python explore_attention_in_rnns.py"

The transformer architecture, introduced by Vaswani et al. in 2017, revolutionized natural language processing. It replaced recurrent connections with self-attention mechanisms, allowing neural networks to capture global dependencies in data, making them highly parallelizable and efficient.

Command: "python explore_transformer_architecture.py"

The core idea behind self-attention is that each element in a sequence can focus on other elements, computing a weighted combination of their representations. This weighted combination allows the network to attend to relevant parts of the input, giving rise to the term "attention."

Command: "python explore_self_attention.py"

Attention mechanisms come in various flavors, such as dot-product attention and scaled dot-product attention, each with its advantages and applications. These mechanisms enable models to learn complex relationships in data and process it effectively.

Command: "python explore_attention_flavors.py"

In natural language processing, attention mechanisms have transformed the field of machine translation. Models like the Transformer have achieved state-of-the-art results by paying selective attention to words in different languages, aligning them, and generating translations.

Command: "python explore_attention_in_translation.py"

Beyond machine translation, attention mechanisms have been applied in tasks like sentiment analysis, text summarization, and question-answering, where they help models focus on the most relevant parts of input data to make accurate predictions.

Command: "python explore_attention_in_nlp_tasks.py"

Computer vision has also seen significant advancements due to attention mechanisms. In image classification, models like the Vision Transformer (ViT) utilize self-attention to process images as sequences of patches, achieving competitive results compared to convolutional neural networks.

Command: "python explore_attention_in_image_classification.py"

In object detection and image segmentation, attention mechanisms enhance the accuracy of models by allowing them to focus on object boundaries and relevant image regions, improving the localization and segmentation of objects.

Command: "python explore_attention_in_object_detection.py"

One of the remarkable aspects of attention mechanisms is their interpretability. Unlike traditional neural networks, attention-based models provide insights into where the model is focusing its attention, making them valuable for applications where model transparency is essential.

Command: "python explore_attention_interpretability.py"

Despite their many successes, attention mechanisms have challenges, such as scalability and computational complexity, which arise when processing long sequences or large-scale datasets. Researchers continue to explore techniques to address these challenges.

Command: "python explore_attention_challenges.py"

Ethical considerations are also vital in the use of attention mechanisms. As models equipped with attention mechanisms gain more capabilities, concerns about their potential biases, privacy implications, and misuse must be carefully addressed.

Command: "python explore_ethical_issues_in_attention.py"

In summary, attention mechanisms have revolutionized deep learning by enabling neural networks to selectively focus on relevant information in data. They have driven advancements in natural language processing, computer vision, and other fields, making models more interpretable and effective. However, ongoing research and ethical considerations will shape the future of attention mechanisms in AI.

Transformer architectures have brought about a revolution in natural language processing (NLP), fundamentally changing the way we approach tasks such as machine translation, text generation, and sentiment analysis. Introduced by Vaswani et al. in their 2017 paper "Attention Is All You Need," the transformer architecture has become the foundation for many state-of-the-art NLP models.

Command: "python explore_transformer_intro.py"

One of the key innovations that transformers introduced was the concept of self-attention mechanisms. Self-attention allows models to weigh the importance of different words in a sentence dynamically, rather than relying on fixed-length context windows as in traditional approaches.

Command: "python explore_self_attention.py"

The transformer architecture is highly parallelizable, making it more computationally efficient than recurrent neural networks (RNNs) and convolutional neural networks (CNNs). This parallelization allows transformers to scale effectively with the size of the training data and the model.

Command: "python explore_transformer_parallelization.py"

In transformers, input sequences are divided into smaller chunks called tokens, which are then processed in parallel. Tokens are embedded into high-dimensional vectors and passed through layers of self-attention and feedforward neural networks to capture complex dependencies within the data.

Command: "python explore_transformer_processing_steps.py"

One of the remarkable features of transformers is their ability to handle sequences of varying lengths. This flexibility is essential for NLP tasks where input text can range from short sentences to lengthy paragraphs.

Command: "python explore_transformer_sequence_length.py"

Transformers have achieved impressive results in machine translation. Models like the original Transformer and its variants, such as BERT and GPT, have pushed the boundaries of translation quality and fluency, outperforming traditional statistical machine translation approaches.

Command: "python explore_transformer_machine_translation.py"

Bidirectional Encoder Representations from Transformers (BERT) introduced the concept of pretraining and fine-tuning in NLP. BERT models are pretrained on large text corpora and then fine-tuned for specific downstream tasks, achieving state-of-the-art performance in tasks like text classification and question answering.

Command: "python explore_bert_pretraining.py"

BERT's masked language modeling objective involves predicting missing words within a sentence, encouraging the model to understand the context and relationships between words. This understanding of context enables BERT to capture rich semantic information.

Command: "python explore_bert_masked_lm.py"

The Generative Pretrained Transformer (GPT) series, on the other hand, focuses on autoregressive language modeling, where the model generates text one word at a time. GPT models have demonstrated their ability to generate coherent and contextually relevant text.

Command: "python explore_gpt_autoregressive.py"

Transformers have found applications in a wide range of NLP tasks, including sentiment analysis, named entity recognition, text summarization, and more. These models can be fine-tuned with smaller datasets to perform well on specific tasks.

Command: "python explore_transformer_nlp_applications.py"

The widespread adoption of transformers in NLP has led to the development of large-scale pretrained models, such as GPT-3, which contains a staggering 175 billion parameters.

These models have pushed the boundaries of NLP performance but also raise concerns about computational resources and ethical considerations.

Command: "python explore_large_pretrained_models.py"

Ethical considerations are essential when developing and deploying transformer-based models. Issues related to bias, fairness, and responsible AI usage must be addressed to ensure that these models benefit society without causing harm.

Command: "python explore_ethical_issues_in_transformers.py"

In summary, transformer architectures have revolutionized natural language processing, enabling models to capture complex dependencies in text data efficiently. From machine translation to text generation, transformers have demonstrated their versatility and effectiveness. However, the responsible development and ethical deployment of these models remain critical as they continue to shape the future of NLP and AI.

Chapter 4: Reinforcement Learning and Deep Q-Networks (DQN)

Reinforcement Learning (RL) is a subfield of artificial intelligence that focuses on developing agents capable of making sequential decisions in an environment to maximize cumulative rewards. Unlike supervised learning, where algorithms learn from labeled data, and unsupervised learning, which deals with uncovering patterns in unlabeled data, RL deals with decision-making in the presence of uncertainty.

Command: "python explore_rl_intro.py"

The core idea behind RL is inspired by how humans and animals learn from interaction with their surroundings. In RL, an agent interacts with an environment, takes actions, receives feedback in the form of rewards, and learns to make better decisions over time.

Command: "python explore_rl_interaction.py"

A fundamental concept in RL is the Markov Decision Process (MDP), which provides a formal framework for modeling decision-making problems. An MDP consists of states, actions, a reward function, and a transition function, all of which define the dynamics of the environment.

Command: "python explore_rl_mdp.py"

The goal of an RL agent is to learn a policy—a mapping from states to actions—that maximizes the expected cumulative reward over time. The policy is the agent's strategy for interacting with the environment.

Command: "python explore_rl_policy.py"

Reinforcement learning agents use various methods to explore and exploit the environment effectively. Exploration involves trying different actions to discover their consequences, while exploitation involves choosing actions that are believed to yield the highest rewards based on current knowledge.

Command: "python explore_rl_exploration.py"

The agent's performance is often evaluated using a performance metric called the return, which represents the sum of rewards obtained during an episode. The goal is to learn a policy that maximizes the expected return over multiple episodes.

Command: "python explore_rl_return.py"

RL algorithms can be categorized into model-free and model-based approaches. Model-free methods directly learn a policy or a value function from interactions with the environment, while model-based methods build an internal model of the environment to plan and make decisions.

Command: "python explore_rl_model_free_vs_model_based.py"

Value-based RL algorithms aim to estimate the expected cumulative reward (value) associated with being in a particular state or taking a specific action. Q-learning and deep Q-networks (DQNs) are examples of popular value-based methods.

Command: "python explore_value_based_rl.py"

Policy-based RL algorithms, on the other hand, focus on learning the policy directly. They parameterize the policy and use techniques like policy gradients to update the policy parameters to maximize expected rewards.

Command: "python explore_policy_based_rl.py"

Actor-Critic methods combine elements of both value-based and policy-based RL. In these algorithms, an actor (policy) learns to select actions, while a critic (value function) estimates the expected cumulative reward.

Command: "python explore_actor_critic_rl.py"

Deep reinforcement learning (DRL) combines RL with deep learning techniques, enabling agents to handle high-dimensional state spaces, such as images or sensor data. DRL has achieved remarkable success in applications like game playing and robotics.
Command: "python explore_deep_rl.py"
Reinforcement learning has found applications in various domains, including autonomous robotics, recommendation systems, finance, healthcare, and gaming. It has demonstrated its potential to solve complex decision-making problems where traditional methods fall short.
Command: "python explore_rl_applications.py"
Ethical considerations in RL are crucial, as agents trained with RL can make decisions that impact human lives. Ensuring fairness, transparency, and accountability in RL systems is a growing concern in the field.
Command: "python explore_ethical_rl.py"
In summary, reinforcement learning is a powerful paradigm for teaching agents to make sequential decisions and learn from their interactions with the environment. It draws inspiration from how humans and animals learn by trial and error, and it has the potential to tackle challenging real-world problems across various domains.

Deep Q-Networks (DQN) have emerged as a significant breakthrough in the field of reinforcement learning, offering a powerful method for training agents to make optimal decisions in various environments.
Command: "python explore_dqn_intro.py"
DQN combines the principles of deep learning with reinforcement learning to enable agents to handle complex, high-dimensional state spaces effectively.
Command: "python explore_dqn_architecture.py"

At the heart of DQN is the Q-learning algorithm, which estimates the value of taking a particular action in a given state. This value is represented by the Q-value, and the goal is to learn the optimal Q-values for all state-action pairs.
Command: "python explore_dqn_q_learning.py"
DQN leverages neural networks to approximate the Q-values, allowing it to generalize across different states and actions.
Command: "python explore_dqn_approximation.py"
One of the key innovations of DQN is the use of experience replay, which stores past experiences (state, action, reward, next state) in a replay buffer and samples mini-batches during training. This technique enhances the stability and efficiency of learning.
Command: "python explore_dqn_experience_replay.py"
Another critical component of DQN is the target network. To stabilize training, DQN maintains two separate neural networks: the online network used for action selection and the target network used to compute target Q-values.
Command: "python explore_dqn_target_network.py"
DQN employs the Bellman equation to update the Q-values iteratively. By minimizing the temporal difference error between the predicted Q-values and target Q-values, the agent gradually learns to make better decisions.
Command: "python explore_dqn_bellman_equation.py"
The success of DQN was demonstrated in the famous Atari 2600 game-playing challenge. DQN agents achieved human-level performance in a range of video games, showcasing their ability to handle diverse and complex environments.
Command: "python explore_dqn_atari_games.py"
DQN's applicability extends beyond gaming. It has been used in robotics, autonomous vehicles, finance, recommendation systems, and healthcare, among other domains.
Command: "python explore_dqn_applications.py"

In robotics, DQN enables robots to learn to perform tasks by interacting with their environment. It has been used for tasks like grasping objects, navigation, and manipulation.
Command: "python explore_dqn_robotics.py"
Autonomous vehicles benefit from DQN for decision-making in complex traffic scenarios, helping ensure safe and efficient driving.
Command: "python explore_dqn_autonomous_vehicles.py"
In finance, DQN aids in portfolio optimization, trading strategy development, and risk management by learning to make informed investment decisions.
Command: "python explore_dqn_finance.py"
Recommendation systems leverage DQN to personalize content and improve user experiences by predicting user preferences and recommending relevant items.
Command: "python explore_dqn_recommendation_systems.py"
In healthcare, DQN has been used for drug discovery, disease diagnosis, and personalized treatment planning, contributing to advancements in medical research and patient care.
Command: "python explore_dqn_healthcare.py"
Despite its successes, DQN has its challenges. Training can be computationally expensive and require substantial amounts of data. Additionally, DQN's effectiveness may be limited in environments with high-dimensional state spaces.
Command: "python explore_dqn_challenges.py"
Ethical considerations are essential in deploying DQN agents in real-world applications, as their decisions can have significant consequences. Ensuring fairness, transparency, and accountability is crucial.
Command: "python explore_dqn_ethical considerations.py"
In summary, Deep Q-Networks have reshaped the field of reinforcement learning and found applications in diverse

domains. Their ability to learn optimal strategies from experience makes them a valuable tool for solving complex decision-making problems. As research continues, DQN is expected to play an even more prominent role in AI-driven applications and technologies.

Chapter 5: Natural Language Processing (NLP) with Deep Learning

Natural Language Processing (NLP) is a field of artificial intelligence that focuses on enabling computers to understand, interpret, and generate human language.
Command: "python explore_nlp_intro.py"
The fundamental goal of NLP is to bridge the gap between human communication and computer understanding, allowing machines to interact with humans in a more natural and intuitive manner.
Command: "python explore_nlp_goal.py"
NLP encompasses a wide range of tasks and applications, from simple text processing and sentiment analysis to complex language understanding and translation.
Command: "python explore_nlp_applications.py"
One of the foundational tasks in NLP is text preprocessing, which involves cleaning and organizing raw text data to make it suitable for analysis.
Command: "python explore_nlp_text_preprocessing.py"
Tokenization, a common text preprocessing step, breaks down text into individual words or tokens, making it easier for computers to work with.
Command: "python explore_nlp_tokenization.py"
Another essential task is part-of-speech tagging, which involves categorizing words in a sentence into their grammatical roles, such as nouns, verbs, and adjectives.
Command: "python explore_nlp_pos_tagging.py"
Named Entity Recognition (NER) is a crucial NLP task that involves identifying and categorizing named entities in text, such as names of people, places, organizations, and more.
Command: "python explore_nlp_ner.py"

Sentiment analysis, also known as opinion mining, is a popular NLP application that determines the sentiment or emotional tone expressed in a piece of text, often classifying it as positive, negative, or neutral.
Command: "python explore_nlp_sentiment_analysis.py"
Machine translation is another critical NLP application, where algorithms are used to automatically translate text from one language to another.
Command: "python explore_nlp_machine_translation.py"
Topic modeling is an unsupervised NLP technique that identifies the main topics present in a collection of documents, helping in document categorization and information retrieval.
Command: "python explore_nlp_topic_modeling.py"
Text generation, a fascinating NLP task, involves training models to generate human-like text, which has applications in chatbots, content generation, and creative writing.
Command: "python explore_nlp_text_generation.py"
NLP leverages various techniques and models, including rule-based methods, statistical models, and deep learning models, to accomplish its tasks.
Command: "python explore_nlp_techniques_and_models.py"
Word embeddings, such as Word2Vec and GloVe, are popular techniques that represent words as dense vectors in continuous space, capturing semantic relationships between words.
Command: "python explore_nlp_word_embeddings.py"
Recurrent Neural Networks (RNNs) are a class of deep learning models widely used in NLP for sequential data processing, allowing them to handle tasks like language modeling and text generation.
Command: "python explore_nlp_rnn.py"

The Transformer architecture, introduced by the "Attention is All You Need" paper, revolutionized NLP by enabling parallel processing of sequences, making it the foundation of models like BERT, GPT, and T5.
Command: "python explore_nlp_transformer.py"
The BERT (Bidirectional Encoder Representations from Transformers) model, pre-trained on massive text corpora, has set new benchmarks in various NLP tasks, achieving state-of-the-art results in natural language understanding.
Command: "python explore_nlp_bert.py"
NLP has made remarkable progress in recent years, with applications spanning chatbots, virtual assistants, sentiment analysis in social media, automated language translation, and healthcare data analysis.
Command: "python explore_nlp_progress_and_applications.py"
However, NLP faces challenges related to ambiguity, context understanding, and cultural nuances, making it an ongoing area of research and development.
Command: "python explore_nlp_challenges.py"
Ethical considerations in NLP are paramount, especially concerning privacy, bias, and fairness, as NLP models can inadvertently perpetuate or amplify societal biases present in training data.
Command: "python explore_nlp_ethical_considerations.py"
In summary, Natural Language Processing is a dynamic field with a wide range of applications, shaping the way we interact with machines and fostering advancements in human-computer communication. NLP continues to evolve, offering exciting opportunities and addressing important challenges in the world of artificial intelligence.

Deep Learning has brought about a significant revolution in

the field of Natural Language Processing (NLP), offering state-of-the-art solutions to a wide range of NLP tasks.

Command: "python explore_dl_for_nlp_intro.py"

One of the key advantages of Deep Learning is its ability to automatically learn and extract meaningful features from raw text data, eliminating the need for extensive manual feature engineering.

Command: "python explore_dl_feature_learning.py"

Recurrent Neural Networks (RNNs) have played a vital role in NLP by allowing models to capture sequential dependencies in text data, making them suitable for tasks like text classification and sentiment analysis.

Command: "python explore_dl_rnns_for_nlp.py"

Long Short-Term Memory (LSTM) networks, a specific type of RNN, have gained popularity for their ability to capture long-range dependencies in text, improving performance in tasks requiring memory.

Command: "python explore_dl_lstm_for_nlp.py"

Gated Recurrent Unit (GRU) networks are another variant of RNNs that are computationally efficient while maintaining the ability to capture sequential patterns.

Command: "python explore_dl_gru_for_nlp.py"

Convolutional Neural Networks (CNNs), known for their success in image processing, have been adapted for NLP tasks by treating text as one-dimensional data and applying convolutions to learn hierarchical features.

Command: "python explore_dl_cnns_for_nlp.py"

Attention mechanisms, introduced by the Transformer model, have revolutionized NLP by enabling models to focus on specific parts of the input sequence, improving performance in tasks like machine translation and text summarization.

Command: "python explore_dl_attention_for_nlp.py"

Transformers, including models like BERT (Bidirectional Encoder Representations from Transformers), have achieved state-of-the-art results in various NLP benchmarks by leveraging large-scale pretraining on massive text corpora.
Command: "python explore_dl_transformers_for_nlp.py"
Transfer learning, a technique where models pretrained on one task are fine-tuned for another, has become a standard approach in NLP, allowing practitioners to achieve excellent results with less data and computation.
Command: "python explore_dl_transfer_learning_for_nlp.py"
Word embeddings, such as Word2Vec and GloVe, are widely used in NLP to represent words as dense vectors, capturing semantic relationships and improving model performance.
Command: "python explore_dl_word_embeddings_for_nlp.py"
Deep Learning models can be applied to various NLP tasks, including but not limited to text classification, sentiment analysis, named entity recognition, machine translation, text summarization, and question-answering.
Command: "python explore_dl_nlp_tasks.py"
The rise of pre-trained language models, like GPT (Generative Pre-trained Transformer), has democratized NLP by providing easy-to-use, off-the-shelf solutions for a wide range of NLP tasks.
Command: "python explore_dl_pretrained_models_for_nlp.py"
Fine-tuning pre-trained models on domain-specific data has become a popular approach for achieving state-of-the-art results in specialized NLP applications, such as legal or medical text analysis.
Command: "python explore_dl_fine_tuning_for_nlp.py"
Multimodal deep learning, which combines text and other data modalities like images or audio, is an emerging field

with applications in areas like content recommendation and sentiment analysis in multimedia content.

Command: "python explore_dl_multimodal_for_nlp.py"

Despite the remarkable successes of Deep Learning in NLP, challenges persist, including handling low-resource languages, addressing bias and fairness concerns, and scaling models to be more efficient and eco-friendly.

Command: "python explore_dl_challenges_in_nlp.py"

Ethical considerations in NLP are crucial, given the potential for models to perpetuate biases present in training data or generate harmful content, making responsible AI development a priority.

Command: "python explore_dl_ethical_considerations_in_nlp.py"

In summary, Deep Learning has revolutionized Natural Language Processing, enabling models to automatically learn complex patterns from text data and achieve remarkable performance across a wide range of NLP tasks. With ongoing research and responsible development, the future holds even more exciting possibilities for Deep Learning in NLP.

Chapter 6: Self-Supervised Learning and Pretraining Strategies

Self-supervised learning is a powerful paradigm in machine learning and deep learning that allows models to learn from unlabeled data, alleviating the need for extensive manual labeling, which can be costly and time-consuming.

Command: "python explore_self_supervised_intro.py"

In self-supervised learning, the process begins by creating a surrogate task or pretext task that generates pseudo-labels from the data without human annotations.

Command: "python explore_self_supervised_pretext_task.py"

For instance, in the context of natural language processing (NLP), a self-supervised model can be trained to predict the missing word in a sentence by utilizing the surrounding words as context.

Command: "python explore_self_supervised_nlp_example.py"

In computer vision, self-supervised models can predict a missing part of an image, such as a masked region, which serves as a pretext task to learn meaningful representations.

Command: "python explore_self_supervised_cv_example.py"

One popular self-supervised learning technique is Contrastive Learning, where the model learns to pull together similar data points and push apart dissimilar ones in an embedding space.

Command: "python explore_self_supervised_contrastive_learning.py"

Another approach is the use of autoencoders, which aim to reconstruct the input data from a compressed representation, encouraging the model to capture essential features.

Command: "python explore_self_supervised_autoencoders.py"

Self-supervised learning has shown remarkable success in various domains, including natural language understanding, computer vision, speech recognition, and recommendation systems.

Command: "python explore_self_supervised_success_stories.py"

Pretraining with self-supervised learning has become a common practice, as it helps initialize models with useful features before fine-tuning them on specific downstream tasks.

Command: "python explore_self_supervised_pretraining.py"

The effectiveness of self-supervised learning lies in its ability to leverage vast amounts of unlabeled data available on the internet, making it a cost-effective and scalable approach.

Command: "python explore_self_supervised_scalability.py"

Contrastive Learning has gained significant attention in recent years, with methods like SimCLR and MoCo achieving impressive results by training on large-scale datasets.

Command: "python explore_self_supervised_contrastive_learning_success.py"

In computer vision, self-supervised models have been applied to tasks such as image classification, object detection, and semantic segmentation, demonstrating state-of-the-art performance.

Command: "python explore_self_supervised_cv_applications.py"

In NLP, self-supervised pretraining has led to breakthroughs in tasks like text classification, question-answering, and language understanding, empowering a wide range of applications.

Command: "python explore_self_supervised_nlp_applications.py"

Despite its success, self-supervised learning is not without challenges, including designing effective pretext tasks, mitigating biases, and fine-tuning models for specific downstream tasks.

Command: "python explore_self_supervised_challenges.py"

Ethical considerations are paramount, as self-supervised models can inadvertently learn biases present in the data they are trained on, potentially reinforcing societal inequalities.

Command: "python explore_self_supervised_ethical_concerns.py"

In summary, self-supervised learning has emerged as a groundbreaking approach in machine learning, enabling models to learn valuable representations from vast amounts of unlabeled data. Its applications span across various domains, from natural language understanding to computer vision, promising more accessible and scalable AI solutions in the future.

Pretraining, also known as pretraining on a large dataset and fine-tuning on a specific task, has become a fundamental and powerful technique in the field of deep learning.

Command: "python explore_pretraining_intro.py"

The concept of pretraining involves training a neural network on a massive, general-purpose dataset, such as ImageNet for computer vision or a large corpus of text for natural language processing.

Command: "python explore_pretraining_large_dataset.py"

During this pretraining phase, the neural network learns to capture essential features and patterns from the vast and diverse data it's exposed to.

Command: "python explore_pretraining_feature_learning.py"

The network effectively learns to represent the data in a way that can be generally useful for a wide range of tasks.

Command: "python explore_pretraining_representation_learning.py"

This learned representation is stored in the neural network's weights and can be transferred to perform various downstream tasks.

Command: "python explore_pretraining_representation_transfer.py"

Transfer learning, enabled by pretraining, allows practitioners to apply a pre-trained model to a specific task with relatively little labeled data.

Command: "python explore_pretraining_transfer_learning.py"

Fine-tuning is the process of taking a pre-trained model and adjusting its parameters to fit the specifics of the target task.

Command: "python explore_pretraining_fine_tuning.py"

Fine-tuning typically involves replacing the final classification layer and updating the weights through backpropagation on the task-specific dataset.

Command: "python explore_pretraining_fine_tuning_process.py"

Pretraining has proven highly effective in various domains. In computer vision, pretraining on ImageNet has led to significant improvements in image classification and object detection tasks.

Command: "python explore_pretraining_cv_success.py"

In natural language processing, models like BERT have demonstrated the power of pretraining on large text corpora, achieving state-of-the-art results in tasks like question-answering and sentiment analysis.

Command: "python explore_pretraining_nlp_success.py"

Audio processing and speech recognition have also benefited from pretraining on vast audio datasets, enabling more accurate speech recognition and audio classification.
Command: "python explore_pretraining_audio_success.py"
Pretraining has extended its reach to reinforcement learning, where agents pre-trained in simulation environments can transfer their learned policies to real-world robotic tasks.
Command: "python explore_pretraining_rl_success.py"
The availability of pre-trained models and their widespread use in open-source libraries, such as Hugging Face Transformers for NLP or TensorFlow Hub for computer vision, has democratized AI development.
Command: "python explore_pretraining_open_source_libraries.py"
One of the key advantages of pretraining is its ability to leverage the enormous amount of unlabeled data available on the internet, making it a cost-effective approach.
Command: "python explore_pretraining_scalability.py"
Despite its successes, pretraining also faces challenges, such as the risk of propagating biases from the large training data or the need for domain adaptation in fine-tuning.
Command: "python explore_pretraining_challenges.py"
Ethical considerations are crucial, as pretraining on large, diverse datasets can inadvertently capture and amplify societal biases present in the data.
Command: "python explore_pretraining_ethical_concerns.py"
In summary, pretraining has become a cornerstone of deep learning, enabling models to harness the knowledge acquired from large, general-purpose datasets to excel in a wide range of specific tasks. Its versatility, scalability, and accessibility make it a pivotal technique in advancing AI and machine learning.

Chapter 7: Advanced Optimization Techniques and Regularization

In the realm of deep learning and machine learning, optimization is a fundamental process that plays a crucial role in training models to make accurate predictions and solve complex tasks.

Command: "python explore_optimization_intro.py"

While gradient descent has been the workhorse of optimization in deep learning, there exist various alternative optimization algorithms that can sometimes outperform gradient descent in terms of convergence speed, stability, and robustness.

Command: "python explore_optimization_alternative_algorithms.py"

One such optimization method is Momentum, which enhances gradient descent by adding a fraction of the previous velocity (accumulated gradients) to the current gradient.

Command: "python explore_optimization_momentum.py"

The inclusion of momentum helps the optimization process overcome small oscillations and accelerate convergence.

Command: "python explore_optimization_momentum_convergence.py"

Another popular optimization technique is RMSprop, which adapts the learning rates for each parameter by dividing the gradient by a running average of squared gradients.

Command: "python explore_optimization_rmsprop.py"

RMSprop can effectively handle non-stationary objectives and converge faster by preventing large oscillations in the optimization process.

Command: "python explore_optimization_rmsprop_convergence.py"

The Adam optimizer combines the advantages of both momentum and RMSprop by maintaining moving averages of both the first-order moment (mean) and second-order moment (uncentered variance) of the gradients.

Command: "python explore_optimization_adam.py"

Adam is known for its robustness and efficiency in a wide range of deep learning tasks.

Command: "python explore_optimization_adam_convergence.py"

Adagrad is another optimization algorithm that adapts the learning rates for each parameter based on the historical gradient information.

Command: "python explore_optimization_adagrad.py"

It is particularly effective in scenarios where some parameters have more sparse updates than others.

Command: "python explore_optimization_adagrad_convergence.py"

The L-BFGS (Limited-memory Broyden-Fletcher-Goldfarb-Shanno) algorithm is a quasi-Newton optimization method that uses approximations of the Hessian matrix to guide the optimization process.

Command: "python explore_optimization_lbfgs.py"

L-BFGS is often used in scenarios where the entire dataset cannot fit in memory.

Command: "python explore_optimization_lbfgs_convergence.py"

The choice of optimization algorithm can significantly impact the training of deep neural networks.

Command: "python explore_optimization_algorithm_choice.py"

In practice, it is common to use adaptive optimizers like Adam or RMSprop, as they tend to work well across a broad range of tasks.

Command: "python explore_optimization_algorithm_choice_best.py"

Hyperparameter tuning is essential when selecting an optimization algorithm, as different algorithms may require different settings for learning rates, momentum values, and other parameters.

Command: "python explore_optimization_hyperparameter_tuning.py"

Furthermore, the availability of powerful hardware accelerators, such as GPUs and TPUs, has also influenced the choice of optimization algorithms, allowing for faster training times and enabling experimentation with various techniques.

Command: "python explore_optimization_hardware_acceleration.py"

It is worth noting that the field of optimization is continuously evolving, with researchers exploring novel techniques and improvements to address the challenges posed by complex deep learning models and large-scale datasets.

Command: "python explore_optimization_future_directions.py"

In summary, while gradient descent remains a fundamental optimization algorithm in deep learning, alternative methods like Momentum, RMSprop, Adam, Adagrad, and L-BFGS offer valuable options for improving convergence, stability, and performance in training deep neural networks. The selection of the most suitable optimization algorithm should consider the specific characteristics of the task, the dataset, and the available hardware resources.

In the world of machine learning and deep learning, overfitting is a common challenge that arises when a model learns to perform exceptionally well on the training data but struggles to generalize its predictions to new, unseen data.
Command: "python explore_regularization_intro.py"
Overfitting occurs when a model becomes too complex and starts capturing noise or idiosyncrasies in the training data, rather than learning the underlying patterns that are truly representative of the problem.
Command: "python explore_regularization_overfitting.py"
To combat overfitting and enhance the generalization ability of models, regularization techniques are employed, which impose constraints or penalties on the model's parameters during training.
Command: "python explore_regularization_concept.py"
One of the most widely used regularization methods is L2 regularization, also known as weight decay, which adds a penalty term to the loss function based on the Euclidean norm (L2 norm) of the model's weights.
Command: "python explore_regularization_l2.py"
L2 regularization encourages the model to keep its weights small, preventing them from growing too large and fitting the noise in the data.
Command: "python explore_regularization_l2_effect.py"
L1 regularization, on the other hand, applies a penalty based on the absolute values of the weights, promoting sparsity in the model.
Command: "python explore_regularization_l1.py"
Sparsity means that some weights become exactly zero, effectively selecting a subset of features and contributing to a simpler model.
Command: "python explore_regularization_l1_effect.py"

Elastic Net regularization combines both L1 and L2 penalties, striking a balance between feature selection and weight decay.

Command: "python explore_regularization_elastic_net.py"

Dropout is a regularization technique specific to neural networks, where random neurons are temporarily "dropped out" during each training iteration.

Command: "python explore_regularization_dropout.py"

This prevents any single neuron from becoming overly reliant on specific features in the training data.

Command: "python explore_regularization_dropout_effect.py"

Dropout is particularly effective in preventing overfitting in deep neural networks and has become a standard practice.

Command: "python explore_regularization_dropout_standard.py"

Another approach is early stopping, where the training process is halted when the model's performance on a validation dataset starts deteriorating.

Command: "python explore_regularization_early_stopping.py"

Early stopping prevents the model from overfitting the training data by monitoring its performance on unseen data.

Command: "python explore_regularization_early_stopping_effect.py"

Data augmentation is a technique used primarily in computer vision, where the training dataset is artificially expanded by applying transformations like rotations, translations, or flips to the input data.

Command: "python explore_regularization_data_augmentation.py"

Data augmentation helps the model generalize better by exposing it to a broader range of variations in the training data.

Command: "python explore_regularization_data_augmentation_effect.py"

Batch normalization is a technique that normalizes the activations within each layer of a neural network, helping stabilize and accelerate training.

Command: "python explore_regularization_batch_normalization.py"

Batch normalization can act as a form of regularization and contribute to mitigating overfitting.

Command: "python explore_regularization_batch_normalization_effect.py"

In the context of deep learning, a novel regularization technique called weight tying or weight sharing has emerged, where weights are shared between different parts of the model, promoting the learning of reusable features.

Command: "python explore_regularization_weight_sharing.py"

Weight sharing encourages the model to discover common patterns in the data and can be particularly effective in tasks like image segmentation or language modeling.

Command: "python explore_regularization_weight_sharing_effect.py"

Hyperparameter tuning is essential when applying regularization techniques, as the choice of hyperparameters, such as the regularization strength or dropout rate, can significantly impact model performance.

Command: "python explore_regularization_hyperparameter_tuning.py"

Ensemble methods, which combine predictions from multiple models, can also act as a form of regularization by reducing the risk of overfitting.

Command: "python explore_regularization_ensembles.py"

In summary, preventing overfitting is a critical concern in machine learning and deep learning, as it ensures that models generalize well to new data. Regularization techniques like L2 and L1 regularization, dropout, early stopping, data augmentation, batch normalization, weight sharing, and ensemble methods play pivotal roles in achieving this goal. The choice of regularization method depends on the specific problem, the dataset, and careful experimentation with hyperparameters to strike the right balance between preventing overfitting and achieving good model performance.

Chapter 8: Interpretability and Explainability in Deep Learning

Interpretability in AI and deep learning is becoming increasingly crucial as these technologies continue to shape our world. Command: "python explore_interpretability_intro.py"

While neural networks and other complex models have achieved remarkable performance in various tasks, they often operate as "black boxes," making it challenging to understand how they arrive at their decisions. Command: "python explore_interpretability_black_box.py"

This lack of transparency raises concerns, especially in critical applications such as healthcare, finance, and autonomous vehicles, where the consequences of errors can be severe. Command: "python explore_interpretability_consequences.py"

Interpretability refers to the ability to explain and understand the inner workings of AI models, shedding light on why they make particular predictions or decisions. Command: "python explore_interpretability_definition.py"

One fundamental aspect of interpretability is feature importance, which helps identify which input features have the most significant influence on the model's output. Command: "python explore_interpretability_feature_importance.py"

Feature importance can assist in identifying critical factors and potential biases within a model. Command: "python explore_interpretability_feature_importance_effect.py"

In the medical field, for instance, an interpretable AI model could provide explanations for a diagnosis, allowing doctors to trust and validate its recommendations. Command: "python explore_interpretability_medical_example.py"

Another aspect of interpretability is model transparency, which involves visualizing the model's internal processes and decision-making. Command: "python explore_interpretability_model_transparency.py"

Techniques like saliency maps and activation maximization can help reveal which parts of an image or text the model focuses on when making predictions. Command: "python explore_interpretability_saliency_maps.py"

Model transparency can improve trust in AI systems and facilitate collaboration between humans and machines. Command: "python explore_interpretability_saliency_maps_effect.py"

In industries like finance, where AI models are used for risk assessment and fraud detection, interpretability can provide regulators and stakeholders with insights into model behavior. Command: "python explore_interpretability_finance_example.py"

Explainable AI (XAI) is an emerging field that aims to develop AI systems explicitly designed to be interpretable. Command: "python explore_interpretability_xai.py"

XAI methods include decision trees, rule-based systems, and simpler neural network architectures. Command: "python explore_interpretability_xai_methods.py"

While XAI techniques offer greater transparency, they may come at the cost of reduced model complexity and performance in some cases. Command: "python explore_interpretability_xai_tradeoff.py"

In ethical and legal contexts, interpretability becomes essential for ensuring fairness, accountability, and transparency (FAT) in AI systems. Command: "python explore_interpretability_ethical_legal.py"

FAT considerations are particularly important when AI systems are involved in sensitive decisions, such as hiring or lending. Command: "python explore_interpretability_ethical_legal_effect.py"

As AI continues to integrate into society, regulatory bodies and policymakers are pushing for guidelines and regulations that emphasize interpretability and responsible AI development. Command: "python explore_interpretability_regulations.py"

In summary, interpretability in AI and deep learning is a critical aspect that bridges the gap between complex models and human understanding. Command: "python explore_interpretability_summary.py"

It ensures that AI systems can be trusted, provides insights into decision-making processes, and aids in addressing ethical and legal concerns. Command: "python explore_interpretability_summary_effect.py"

Balancing the need for high-performance models with interpretability will be an ongoing challenge, but it's a necessary one to harness the full potential of AI while maintaining transparency and accountability.

Explainable AI (XAI) techniques and approaches have gained significant prominence in the field of artificial intelligence, addressing the need for transparency and interpretability in complex machine learning models. Command: "python explore_xai_intro.py"

The increasing adoption of AI in critical domains such as healthcare, finance, and autonomous vehicles has underscored the importance of understanding how AI systems arrive at their decisions. Command: "python explore_xai_importance.py"

XAI refers to a set of methods and tools designed to make AI models more transparent, interpretable, and accountable. Command: "python explore_xai_definition.py"

One of the fundamental concepts in XAI is the notion of model transparency, which involves making the inner workings of an AI model more accessible to humans. Command: "python explore_xai_model_transparency.py"

Model transparency can be achieved through techniques such as decision trees, rule-based models, and simplified neural network architectures. Command: "python explore_xai_model_transparency_methods.py"

While these methods may sacrifice some level of complexity and performance, they offer the advantage of providing clear and understandable explanations for model decisions. Command: "python explore_xai_model_transparency_tradeoff.py"

Another critical aspect of XAI is feature importance, which helps identify the most influential input features in a model's decision-making process. Command: "python explore_xai_feature_importance.py"

Feature importance is particularly valuable in scenarios where understanding which variables drive model predictions is crucial. Command: "python explore_xai_feature_importance_effect.py"

One of the widely used techniques for understanding model predictions is Local Interpretable Model-agnostic Explanations (LIME). Command: "python explore_xai_lime.py"

LIME generates locally faithful explanations by perturbing input data and observing how the model's predictions change. Command: "python explore_xai_lime_example.py"

Interpretable Machine Learning (IML) is a framework within XAI that focuses on building models with inherent interpretability. Command: "python explore_xai_iml.py"

IML models, such as generalized linear models and decision trees, provide interpretable outputs without the need for post-hoc explanations. Command: "python explore_xai_iml_methods.py"

Ethical and legal considerations are driving the adoption of XAI in industries where AI systems make impactful decisions, like credit scoring or hiring. Command: "python explore_xai_ethical_legal.py"

XAI helps ensure fairness, accountability, and transparency (FAT) in AI applications, reducing the risk of biased or discriminatory outcomes. Command: "python explore_xai_ethical_legal_effect.py"

Counterfactual explanations are a powerful XAI technique that provides users with alternative scenarios to understand the impact of different inputs on model decisions. Command: "python explore_xai_counterfactuals.py"

These counterfactuals can be valuable in contexts where users want to know how to achieve a desired model outcome or avoid an undesired one. Command: "python explore_xai_counterfactuals_example.py"

In summary, XAI techniques and approaches play a pivotal role in bridging the gap between complex AI models and human understanding. Command: "python explore_xai_summary.py"

They are instrumental in building trust, ensuring fairness, and meeting regulatory requirements in AI applications across various industries. Command: "python explore_xai_summary_effect.py"

As the demand for transparent and interpretable AI continues to grow, XAI will remain at the forefront of research and development, striving to strike a balance between model performance and human comprehensibility. Command: "python explore_xai_future_directions.py"

Chapter 9: Ethics, Bias, and Fairness in AI and Deep Learning

Addressing bias and fairness concerns in AI is a critical and evolving aspect of artificial intelligence that encompasses both technological and ethical dimensions. Command: "python explore_bias_fairness_intro.py"

Bias in AI systems refers to the presence of systematic and unfair discrimination in their decision-making processes, often resulting in unequal treatment of different groups or individuals. Command: "python explore_bias_fairness_definition.py"

This bias can manifest in various forms, such as gender bias, racial bias, and socio-economic bias, among others, and can have serious real-world consequences. Command: "python explore_bias_fairness_examples.py"

One of the fundamental challenges in mitigating bias is the collection and labeling of training data, which can inadvertently reflect societal biases present in historical data. Command: "python explore_bias_fairness_training_data.py"

Data preprocessing and cleaning techniques, such as re-sampling underrepresented groups or using de-biasing algorithms, are crucial steps in addressing bias at the dataset level. Command: "python explore_bias_fairness_data_preprocessing.py"

However, mitigating bias at the data level is just the beginning; model training and evaluation also play pivotal roles in ensuring fairness in AI systems. Command: "python explore_bias_fairness_model_training.py"

Fairness-aware machine learning algorithms aim to optimize model performance while considering fairness constraints to minimize disparate impact. Command: "python explore_bias_fairness_fairness_aware.py"

Metrics like demographic parity and equal opportunity are commonly used to quantify fairness and guide model training and evaluation. Command: "python explore_bias_fairness_fairness_metrics.py"

Fairness constraints can be integrated into optimization objectives to explicitly address and reduce bias during model training. Command: "python explore_bias_fairness_fairness_constraints.py"

Explainability and interpretability in AI models are crucial for understanding and detecting bias, as they allow stakeholders to analyze model decisions and identify sources of bias. Command: "python explore_bias_fairness_explainability.py"

Ethical considerations in AI development emphasize the importance of involving diverse teams and stakeholders, conducting bias audits, and maintaining transparency throughout the development process. Command: "python explore_bias_fairness_ethical_guidelines.py"

Regulatory frameworks, such as the General Data Protection Regulation (GDPR) and the Fair Credit Reporting Act (FCRA), require organizations to be transparent about AI-driven decisions and provide individuals with recourse in case of bias-related harm. Command: "python explore_bias_fairness_regulatory_frameworks.py"

Addressing bias and fairness concerns in AI is an ongoing process that requires collaboration across disciplines, including computer science, ethics, law, and social sciences. Command: "python explore_bias_fairness_collaborative_approach.py"

The deployment of AI systems must be accompanied by continuous monitoring and auditing to detect and rectify bias that may emerge in real-world scenarios. Command: "python explore_bias_fairness_continuous_monitoring.py"

Public awareness and advocacy for fair AI systems are essential in holding organizations accountable and driving positive changes in the AI industry. Command: "python explore_bias_fairness_public_advocacy.py"

In summary, addressing bias and fairness concerns in AI is not only a technological challenge but also a moral imperative. Command: "python explore_bias_fairness_conclusion.py"

It requires a multi-faceted approach that combines technical advancements, ethical principles, regulatory frameworks, and social awareness to ensure that AI systems benefit all of humanity fairly and equitably. Command: "python explore_bias_fairness_future_directions.py"

Ethical considerations in deep learning research are of paramount importance, guiding the development and application of AI technologies in ways that align with human values and societal well-being. Command: "python explore_ethical_intro.py"

Deep learning, with its remarkable capabilities, has the potential to revolutionize various fields, but it also raises ethical dilemmas that must be addressed responsibly. Command: "python explore_ethical_potential_impact.py"

One central ethical concern is the potential for AI algorithms to perpetuate or even amplify existing biases present in the data they are trained on. Command: "python explore_ethical_bias_in_ai.py"

To tackle this challenge, researchers and developers must prioritize fairness and strive to reduce bias in AI systems, ensuring that they do not discriminate against particular groups or individuals. Command: "python explore_ethical_mitigating_bias.py"

Another critical ethical consideration is transparency in AI decision-making, as opaque algorithms can lead to a lack of accountability and trust among users and stakeholders. Command: "python explore_ethical_transparency.py"

Research efforts in explainable AI (XAI) aim to address this issue by making AI models more interpretable, allowing users to understand why a particular decision was made. Command: "python explore_ethical_xai.py"

Privacy concerns also loom large, as AI systems can potentially infringe on individuals' privacy rights by analyzing personal data without consent or knowledge. Command: "python explore_ethical_privacy.py"

Stricter data protection regulations, such as the European Union's General Data Protection Regulation (GDPR), provide a framework for safeguarding data privacy and holding organizations accountable for how they handle personal information. Command: "python explore_ethical_gdpr.py"

The ethical use of AI extends beyond privacy and fairness to encompass issues like accountability and responsibility for AI-driven decisions. Command: "python explore_ethical_accountability.py"

Ethical guidelines and codes of conduct are emerging to provide a framework for AI researchers, developers, and organizations to navigate the ethical landscape. Command: "python explore_ethical_guidelines.py"

Responsible AI development involves considering the potential consequences of AI applications and conducting ethical impact assessments to evaluate the risks and benefits. Command: "python explore_ethical_impact_assessment.py"

Another dimension of ethical consideration is AI's impact on employment, with concerns about job displacement due to automation and the responsibility to provide reskilling and upskilling opportunities for affected workers. Command: "python explore_ethical_employment_impact.py"

AI researchers also grapple with dual-use concerns, where AI technologies developed for benign purposes may be misused for harmful activities, emphasizing the need for ethical vigilance and safeguards. Command: "python explore_ethical_dual_use.py"

International collaboration and dialogue among researchers, policymakers, and civil society organizations are essential to establish global norms and ethical standards for AI development and deployment. Command: "python explore_ethical_international_collaboration.py"

In summary, ethical considerations in deep learning research are inseparable from the advancement of AI technologies. Command: "python explore_ethical_conclusion.py"

By addressing these ethical challenges and fostering a culture of responsible AI development, the field can harness its potential while ensuring that AI benefits society at large and upholds fundamental ethical principles. Command: "python explore_ethical_future_directions.py"

Chapter 10: Cutting-Edge Applications of Deep Learning in Healthcare, Finance, and Beyond

Deep learning is making profound strides in revolutionizing the healthcare industry, offering innovative solutions to long-standing challenges and ushering in an era of transformative possibilities. Command: "python explore_healthcare_intro.py"

At its core, deep learning leverages neural networks, inspired by the human brain's structure, to process and analyze vast amounts of medical data with remarkable accuracy. Command: "python explore_healthcare_neural_networks.py"

One of the most promising applications of deep learning in healthcare is medical image analysis, where algorithms can diagnose diseases from X-rays, MRIs, and CT scans with unprecedented precision. Command: "python explore_healthcare_image_analysis.py"

Radiology, for example, has witnessed substantial improvements in the detection of anomalies such as tumors, fractures, and abnormalities through deep learning-powered diagnostic tools. Command: "python explore_healthcare_radiology_advancements.py"

In addition to diagnostics, deep learning is poised to enhance medical treatment planning and optimization, tailoring therapies to individual patient profiles. Command: "python explore_healthcare_treatment_optimization.py"

Drug discovery, a traditionally labor-intensive process, benefits from deep learning by predicting potential drug candidates and accelerating the development of new medications. Command: "python explore_healthcare_drug_discovery.py"

The integration of electronic health records (EHRs) with deep learning systems allows healthcare providers to gain insights from patient data, improving care coordination and patient outcomes. Command: "python explore_healthcare_ehrs.py"
Natural language processing (NLP) models are enabling the extraction of valuable information from unstructured medical texts, helping clinicians make more informed decisions. Command: "python explore_healthcare_nlp.py"
In the realm of genomics, deep learning plays a pivotal role in deciphering genetic codes and identifying genetic markers associated with diseases, advancing personalized medicine. Command: "python explore_healthcare_genomics.py"
Chronic disease management stands to benefit from continuous monitoring through wearable devices and sensors, where deep learning algorithms can detect early signs of deterioration. Command: "python explore_healthcare_wearables.py"
Telemedicine is experiencing a surge in popularity, with deep learning aiding in remote patient monitoring, diagnosis, and treatment, particularly during global health crises. Command: "python explore_healthcare_telemedicine.py"
The ability to predict disease outbreaks and track their spread is becoming increasingly crucial, and deep learning models are being employed for epidemiological forecasting. Command: "python explore_healthcare_epidemiology.py"
While the present applications of deep learning in healthcare are impressive, the future holds even more promise. Command: "python explore_healthcare_future_promise.py"
Personalized treatment plans, tailored to an individual's genetic makeup and medical history, are on the horizon, potentially transforming the way we approach healthcare. Command: "python explore_healthcare_personalized_treatment.py"

AI-driven virtual health assistants, capable of providing medical advice and monitoring patients in real-time, are expected to become integral to healthcare delivery. Command: "python explore_healthcare_virtual_assistants.py"

The democratization of healthcare through AI-powered tools empowers patients to take a proactive role in their well-being, fostering a shift toward preventive medicine. Command: "python explore_healthcare_democratization.py"

However, ethical considerations in healthcare AI are paramount, as the handling of sensitive patient data and the potential for bias in algorithms must be carefully managed. Command: "python explore_healthcare_ethical_considerations.py"

Interoperability of healthcare systems and data sharing among institutions pose challenges that must be addressed to fully realize the potential of deep learning in healthcare. Command: "python explore_healthcare_interoperability.py"

Regulatory frameworks and standards for AI in healthcare are evolving, with regulatory bodies working to ensure the safety and efficacy of AI-driven medical technologies. Command: "python explore_healthcare_regulation.py"

The collaboration between AI experts, healthcare professionals, and policymakers is pivotal in shaping the responsible and equitable adoption of deep learning in healthcare. Command: "python explore_healthcare_collaboration.py"

In summary, the convergence of deep learning and healthcare promises to redefine the industry, improving patient care, accelerating medical research, and enhancing healthcare accessibility. Command: "python explore_healthcare_conclusion.py"

As we navigate this transformative journey, it is imperative to strike a balance between innovation and ethics, ensuring that the future of healthcare remains both cutting-edge and compassionate. Command: "python explore_healthcare_future_directions.py

Financial forecasting and risk management are two critical components of modern finance, and the integration of deep learning techniques is reshaping how these processes are conducted. Command: "python explore_finance_intro.py"

Deep learning, with its ability to analyze vast amounts of data and detect complex patterns, has emerged as a powerful tool for predicting financial market movements. Command: "python explore_finance_deep_learning.py"

One of the key challenges in financial forecasting is predicting stock prices, and deep learning models like recurrent neural networks (RNNs) and long short-term memory (LSTM) networks have shown promising results in this domain. Command: "python explore_finance_stock_forecasting.py"

Cryptocurrency markets, known for their extreme volatility, can also benefit from deep learning-based forecasting models, aiding traders and investors in decision-making. Command: "python explore_finance_crypto_forecasting.py"

Risk management is a fundamental aspect of financial institutions, and deep learning contributes by identifying and mitigating risks more effectively. Command: "python explore_finance_risk_management.py"

Credit risk assessment, a critical task for banks, can be improved with deep learning algorithms that analyze customer data and credit histories to predict default probabilities. Command: "python explore_finance_credit_risk.py"

Fraud detection in financial transactions is another area where deep learning shines, as it can quickly detect anomalies and potentially fraudulent activities. Command: "python explore_finance_fraud_detection.py"

Portfolio management benefits from deep reinforcement learning, which helps optimize investment strategies by considering various factors and market dynamics. Command: "python explore_finance_portfolio_management.py"

Algorithmic trading, an integral part of financial markets, leverages deep learning models to make high-frequency trading decisions based on real-time data. Command: "python explore_finance_algorithmic_trading.py"

Regulatory compliance in finance can be enhanced with deep learning tools that monitor transactions and ensure adherence to financial regulations. Command: "python explore_finance_regulatory_compliance.py"

However, the implementation of deep learning in finance comes with its set of challenges, including the need for vast amounts of quality data, model interpretability, and ethical considerations. Command: "python explore_finance_challenges.py"

The availability of historical financial data, combined with advances in computing power, has enabled the development of increasingly sophisticated deep learning models for financial forecasting. Command: "python explore_finance_data_availability.py"

Model interpretability is crucial in financial applications, as stakeholders need to understand how predictions are made and assess the risk associated with model decisions. Command: "python explore_finance_interpretability.py"

Ethical concerns, such as bias in financial algorithms and the responsible use of AI in finance, have gained prominence and require careful consideration. Command: "python explore_finance_ethical_concerns.py"

Collaboration between finance experts and data scientists is essential to harness the full potential of deep learning in finance while addressing these challenges. Command: "python explore_finance_collaboration.py"

In the future, deep learning is expected to further disrupt traditional finance, with applications extending to credit scoring, insurance, and even central banking. Command: "python explore_finance_future_applications.py"

Central banks may use deep learning models to inform monetary policy decisions, leveraging the power of AI to navigate complex economic landscapes. Command: "python explore_finance_central_banking.py"

The democratization of finance through AI-driven fintech startups is democratizing access to financial services, making them more inclusive and efficient. Command: "python explore_finance_democratization.py"

In summary, the integration of deep learning in financial forecasting and risk management has the potential to revolutionize the industry, providing more accurate predictions and better risk assessment. Command: "python explore_finance_conclusion.py"

As finance continues to embrace the power of deep learning, it is crucial to strike a balance between innovation and responsible, ethical practices, ensuring a sustainable and secure financial future. Command: "python explore_finance_responsible_practices.py"

Conclusion

In this comprehensive book bundle, "DEEP LEARNING: COMPUTER VISION, PYTHON MACHINE LEARNING AND NEURAL NETWORKS," we embarked on a journey through the exciting world of artificial intelligence and deep learning. Across the four distinct books, we explored a wide spectrum of topics, from the fundamentals to the cutting-edge techniques and applications of deep learning.

"BOOK 1 - DEEP LEARNING DEMYSTIFIED: A BEGINNER'S GUIDE" served as our stepping stone into the realm of deep learning. Here, we laid the foundation for understanding neural networks, activation functions, and the basics of Python programming. With clear explanations and practical examples, beginners were introduced to the fascinating world of AI.

"BOOK 2 - MASTERING COMPUTER VISION WITH DEEP LEARNING" took us on an exhilarating journey into the realm of computer vision. We delved into image processing, convolutional neural networks (CNNs), and object detection, equipping readers with the knowledge to create intelligent vision-based applications. From recognizing objects to semantic segmentation, this book made us masters of visual understanding.

"BOOK 3 - PYTHON MACHINE LEARNING AND NEURAL NETWORKS: FROM NOVICE TO PRO" expanded our horizons by exploring the world of machine learning and neural networks. We learned the art of data preprocessing, supervised and unsupervised learning techniques, and the intricacies of training powerful neural networks. From novices to proficient practitioners, this book catered to learners at every stage.

"BOOK 4 - ADVANCED DEEP LEARNING: CUTTING-EDGE TECHNIQUES AND APPLICATIONS" was our gateway to the future of deep learning. We explored advanced optimization techniques, transfer learning, and the critical aspects of overcoming common deep learning challenges. The book concluded with a glimpse into the real-world applications and emerging trends in deep learning, showcasing the limitless potential of this field.

Throughout this journey, we gained insights into the evolving landscape of deep learning, its role in computer vision, its applications in natural language processing, and its significance in healthcare, finance, and beyond. We also grappled with the ethical considerations, interpretability challenges, and the need for fairness in AI and deep learning.

As we conclude this book bundle, it's important to recognize that deep learning is not merely a technological phenomenon; it's a transformative force reshaping industries, economies, and societies. Whether you are a beginner seeking to demystify deep learning or an expert diving into cutting-edge techniques, this bundle has provided you with the knowledge and tools to navigate the ever-changing landscape of AI.

The journey doesn't end here; it's a continuous exploration of the possibilities that deep learning offers. The future holds countless opportunities for innovation, and with the knowledge gained from these books, you are well-equipped to contribute to the ever-evolving field of deep learning.

Thank you for joining us on this enlightening journey, and may your endeavors in the world of AI and deep learning be filled with success and meaningful impact.

www.ingramcontent.com/pod-product-compliance
Lightning Source LLC
Chambersburg PA
CBHW071234050326
40690CB00011B/2115